POWERFUL
PRAYERS
THAT OPEN
HEAVEN

POWERFUL
PRAYERS
THAT OPEN
HEAVEN

JAMIE T. PLEASANT

WHITAKER
HOUSE

Powerful Prayers That Open Heaven

Jamie T. Pleasant, Ph.D.
www.newzionchristianchurch.org
jpleasant@kingdombuilders.org
3145 Old Atlanta Rd.
Suwanee, GA 30024

ISBN: 978-1-62911-952-6
eBook ISBN: 978-1-62911-953-3
Printed in the United States of America
© 2018 by Jamie T. Pleasant

Whitaker House
1030 Hunt Valley Circle
New Kensington, PA 15068
www.whitakerhouse.com

Library of Congress Cataloging-in-Publication Data (Pending)

1 2 3 4 5 6 7 8 9 10 11 **W** 25 24 23 22 21 20 19 18

DEDICATION

To my daddy, Anthony T. Pleasant, who was a perfect example to me of a real man. I will never forget the sacrifices and personal time you spent with me as a child. Daddy, I am still trying to live up to the perfect example of a father that you were to me. Rest in peace!

To my wife, Kimberly (God gave me His best in you!), my two sons Christian and Zion, and daughter, Nacara. You all are the wind beneath my wings. All I want to do is leave a legacy of Godliness to you.

To everyone that made a positive impact in my life. If I have forgotten anyone, please charge it to my old age and not my heart.

Humbly yours,
Jamie

CONTENTS

FOREWORD

Powerful Prayers That Open Heaven, by my very good friend, Dr. Jamie Pleasant, is indeed powerful. I have read several of Jamie's books and am happy to have this one added to my collection. This book will change your prayer life by clearly explaining what happens during the prayer process. It is a good reminder of the power made available to us when we pray. Dr. Pleasant goes into detail about the different stages of prayer and shows the reader how heaven is engaged in our daily prayers.

Dr. Pleasant has spoken at several chapel meetings during my time at Clemson, and I have truly enjoyed his motivational and inspirational messages. I have been challenged and encouraged by the way God speaks through him. He always reminds me that I have a purpose in this life that exceeds football, work, and earthly accolades.

I have enjoyed all of Jamie's books, but this is one I recommend for everyone, at all levels of life. I have no doubt this book will strengthen your devotional life and change the way you think about prayer.

—*Dabo Swinney*
Head football coach, Clemson University
ALL IN.

GETTING THE MOST FROM *POWERFUL PRAYERS THAT OPEN HEAVEN*

Get ready to take your prayer life to the next level. You can use this book for personal or group study. The nine chapters in this book are perfect for a week-by-week study for groups or individuals. Eight of the chapters include key truths that will show you how to open the gates of heaven when you pray. The last chapter recaps what you've learned.

In addition, you'll find key points in each chapter and exercises at the end of each chapter. The key points are set off from the rest of the chapter in bold and are reinforced at the end of the chapter. The journaling spaces allow you to write down your thoughts and reflect on key points within the chapter. Completing the exercises within the chapter and at the end of each chapter will help you to reinforce what you have learned.

1

WHEN WE PRAY, HEAVEN OPENS UP

One of the greatest secrets of prayer in the Bible is revealed in Luke 3:21:

> When all the people were being baptized, Jesus was baptized too. And as he was praying, heaven was opened.

As Christ Jesus was praying, "heaven was opened." What a revelation for us to know that every single time we pray, heaven opens up, right in front of our eyes!

The first thing we must do in order to begin to have a more productive prayer life is to envision that as we pray, heaven opens up for us. Take a moment and look up, wherever you are. I want you to visualize heaven opening up. As hard as it may be to believe, according to Scripture, that is exactly what happens when you pray. The main point of this exercise, however, is for you to know that what you envision becomes a reality in your prayer life. The first training you must undergo in order to become a powerful person of prayer is to begin to see through visioning exercises that heaven does actually open up. Envisioning is the key to unlocking the supernatural world of prayer and the things of God.

> **ENVISIONING IS THE KEY TO UNLOCKING THE SUPERNATURAL WORLD OF PRAYER AND THE THINGS OF GOD.**

Try this exercise for starters. Look at the cube below. Don't just look at it for an instant. Stare at it without interruption for at least forty-five seconds. Don't move your eyes off of it. Go ahead and start now.

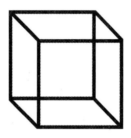

Did you notice anything peculiar? You should have. Write down what you saw as you focused on the cube.

_____

_____

_____

_____

_____

_____

The openings of the cube should have changed. The cube may have even shifted positions on the paper right in front of your eyes. It might have even turned around completely as you stared at it. At first, you may have seen an opening at the top. Then, as you continued to stare at it, it may have shifted to the left, right, or bottom. Did that happen to you? If not, go back and practice this envisioning exercise. Until you can look at this still image on paper and see it move, you are not ready to see heaven open up when you look to the sky while you are praying.

That's right, heaven opens up, and it has always opened up, but we must know that it happens and see that it happens in order for effective, powerful prayer to occur in our lives. An important concept to understand is that for supernatural things to manifest in our world through prayer, we must visualize them with our natural eyes before they occur. *Did you get that?* It sounds counter-intuitive, but we must be able to visualize supernatural things with our natural eyes, things the naked eye normally can't see.

We must train ourselves to see that which is always there, that which has always been there, and that which will always be there. These are things normal eyes can't see without the help of the Holy Spirit. If we can begin to visualize spiritual things with our natural eyes, they will become a reality in our natural life.

> **IF WE CAN BEGIN TO VISUALIZE SPIRITUAL THINGS WITH OUR NATURAL EYES, THEY WILL BECOME A REALITY IN OUR NATURAL LIFE.**

Take a look at 2 Corinthians 4:18:

So we fix our eyes not on what is seen, but on what is unseen, since what is seen is temporary, but what is unseen is eternal.

What a powerful Scripture for us! Notice God's truth here. We are not creating something that is not there. Scripture says that it has *always* been there, waiting for us to focus on it long enough so that it becomes a reality. Let's dig deeper. According to this verse, we should focus on the eternal things of God, which are permanent, and not easily seen with natural eyes.

What a blessing it is to know that there is a permanent reality waiting for us beyond the temporary realm we now experience in our daily lives. To make this point clearer, think about some of the many problems you may be focusing on in your life—bills, car problems, an exam, loneliness, health problems, etc. All the trials and challenges we face each day are only temporary, not permanent.

> ALL THE TRIALS AND CHALLENGES WE FACE EACH DAY
> ARE ONLY TEMPORARY, NOT PERMANENT.

But God's voice, presence, blessings, love, peace, and power—things we can't seem to put our hands on—are eternal.

> GOD'S VOICE, PRESENCE, BLESSINGS,
> LOVE, PEACE, AND POWER—THINGS WE CAN'T SEEM
> TO PUT OUR HANDS ON—ARE ETERNAL.

In this next exercise, I want you to reflect upon the amount of time you spend focusing on your trials, and upon the amount of time you spend focusing on God. In the spaces provided, write down the number of minutes or hours you spend focusing on each of these things on a daily basis.

I usually spend _____ a day experiencing trouble in my life.

I usually spend _____ a day focusing on a solution to the trouble in my life.

I usually spend _____ a day experiencing the goodness, blessing, and power of God in my life.

I usually spend _____ a day praying to God that His blessings will be revealed in my life.

How did you do with the exercise? Did you discover that you spend more time experiencing and focusing on problems and on how to solve them than you do on the goodness of God and on His blessings? If so, it may be that part of the reason you are struggling so much with problems and heartaches is because you focus on *them* more than you focus on *God*. We must focus and desperately look for the unseen yet permanent things from God.

PART OF THE REASON YOU ARE STRUGGLING SO MUCH WITH PROBLEMS AND HEARTACHES IS BECAUSE YOU FOCUS ON *THEM* MORE THAN YOU FOCUS ON *GOD*.

We need to recognize that the things we focus on most tend to become our reality. In the midst of painful and troubling events, we need to focus on the goodness of God. Philippians 4:8 says,

Finally, brothers and sisters, whatever is true, whatever is noble, whatever is right, whatever is pure, whatever is lovely, whatever is admirable—if anything is excellent or praiseworthy—think about such things.

We must now begin to tap into the power of prayer and access the unseen realm of blessings. And as we pray, we need to see heaven open up for us, releasing beautiful things like peace, joy, patience, and power. What a blessing it will be when, in the middle of trying times, we can step back and go to a place of eternal bliss, even in the midst of heartache, pain, and trouble. This place is not imagined. This place is *real*, and it is called *prayer*.

THE THINGS WE FOCUS ON MOST TEND TO BECOME OUR REALITY.

Looking back at Luke 3:21, we see Christ Jesus praying and heaven opening. He is about to begin His earthly mission. He needs to know for certain that His Father is with Him. He needs to know that He has been given power through the Holy Spirit to be successful. He needs to know that as He experiences resistance and trouble from His enemies, He will be delivered. He needs to know that His outcome will be assured before He steps out. Thus, as He is being baptized and begins to pray, He watches eagerly for assurance that His time and protection have truly come. He can't rely on guesswork. He doesn't want to depend on false hope or fleeting dreams. Christ Jesus must know that He is walking in divine purpose and protection, and that it is time for Him to begin His mission on earth.

As Jesus enters into prayer, He focuses so intently on heaven that He sees it open, and then He hears the voice of His Father:

And as he was praying, heaven was opened and the Holy Spirit descended on him in bodily form like a dove. And a voice came from heaven: "You are my Son, whom I love; with you I am well pleased."   (Luke 3:21–22)

According to Scripture, Jesus never said a word. He was looking toward heaven, and all of a sudden, it opened up for Him and He heard the voice of His Father. A major breakthrough in understanding prayer is that there should be less talking by us and more listening to Him.

> **A MAJOR BREAKTHROUGH IN UNDERSTANDING PRAYER IS THAT THERE SHOULD BE LESS TALKING BY US AND MORE LISTENING TO HIM.**

What a powerful prayer life Christ Jesus must have had to be able to stand up, focus on heaven, envision spiritual realities, and then hear the voice of His Father. But here's an incredible spiritual truth: we too can get to the place where we stand up, focus on heaven, envision it opening up before us, and then begin to hear the voice of our heavenly Father. It *can* happen. All we have to do is focus, envision, and wait. Let's continue on in our prayer journey.

CHAPTER 1: KEY POINT REVIEW

Let's review the key points of this chapter.

1. When we pray, heaven opens up for us.

2. Envisioning is the key to unlocking the supernatural world of prayer and the things of God.

3. If we can't see spiritual things with our natural eyes, they will never become a reality in our natural life.

4. Problems, troubles, and challenges we see and face daily are temporary, not permanent.

5. God's voice, presence, blessings, love, peace, and power—things we can't seem to put our hands on—are eternal.

6. Part of the reason why you are struggling so much with your problems and heartaches is because you focus on *them* more than you focus on *God*.

7. Our reality becomes what we focus on, and what we focus on becomes our reality.

8. A major breakthrough in understanding prayer is that there should be less talking by us and more listening to Him.

9. We must get to the stage in which we can stand up, focus on heaven, envision it opening up before us, and then wait for the voice of the Father to speak to us.

SPIRITUAL EXERCISE

1. Write a prayer to God. Ask Him to give you the ability to focus on heaven, to envision spiritual realities, and to wait on Him to speak as heaven opens up to you.

_____

_____

_____

_____

_____

_____

_____

2. Next, quiet yourself, look up to heaven, and envision it opening. Wait and be patient. Write down what God says to you.

_____

_____

_____

_____

_____

_____

_____

_____

2

PRAYER CHANGES THINGS, AND YOU SHOULD CHANGE, TOO

As he was praying, the appearance of his face changed, and
his clothes became as bright as a flash of lightning.
—Luke 9:29

If you were to ask your family members, friends, coworkers, and even fellow church members if they believe that prayer changes things, the majority of them would most likely agree. However, if you were to ask whether they believe that prayer can change things during the actual prayer experience, you might get a different response. While most people are confident in the concept that prayer can change their situations and circumstances, their confidence becomes more cautious when it comes to their expectation of witnessing that change *while* they are praying.

Praise God, there is great news concerning the time that we spend with God in prayer. The good news is that as we pray, change immediately begins to have a positive impact on our situations and circumstances.

Also, it is important for us to know that when we are in the act of praying, our prayers have a profound and positive impact on our spirits, minds, souls, and bodies.

> ## AS WE PRAY, CHANGE IMMEDIATELY BEGINS TO HAVE A POSITIVE IMPACT ON OUR SITUATIONS AND CIRCUMSTANCES.

Take a look at Luke 9:28–29:

> *About eight days after Jesus said this, he took Peter, John and James with him and went up onto a mountain to pray. **As he was praying**, the appearance of his face changed, and his clothes became as bright as a flash of lightning.*

Jesus was about to let Peter, John, and James in on one of the greatest secrets about prayer. Many times in the Bible, we see Christ go off alone to pray. However, there is something different about His prayer time in this Scripture. He wants them to watch and learn how He enters into prayer, and He wants them to understand the benefits of such a deep involvement in the prayer activity.

> ## OUR PRAYERS HAVE A PROFOUND AND POSITIVE IMPACT ON OUR SPIRITS, MINDS, SOULS, AND BODIES.

THE NINE PRAYER POINTS OF COMPLETENESS

In Luke 9:29, the key words we should focus on are "*as he was praying.*" It was "*as he was praying*" that the appearance of His face changed. This is a beautiful example to help us rethink the way we approach and conduct personal prayer. As we pray, we should expect, at the very least, our face or our disposition to change. It is not Christ's intent to teach us and show us what *might* happen *after* we pray. It is His purpose to show us what *will* happen *as* we are praying. It is His intent to show us what takes place every time we pray.

We should have a confident expectation that one of the first things to change during our personal prayer time is our disposition. Our *disposition* is "the predominant or prevailing tendency of one's spirits; natural mental and emotional outlook or mood; characteristic attitude."[1] The power in this definition is in the progressive unfolding it describes. This is part of what I call the "Nine Prayer Points of Completeness" that take place within us as we pray, and that have a direct effect on how we respond to things in our daily lives.

GOD'S PRESENCE, OUR SPIRIT, OUR NATURAL BODY, OUR MENTAL STATE, OUR EMOTIONAL STATE, OUR OUTLOOK ON LIFE, OUR MOOD, OUR CHARACTER, AND OUR ATTITUDE MAKE UP THE NINE PRAYER POINTS OF COMPLETENESS THAT MUST UNFOLD IN ORDER FOR POSITIVE CHANGE TO TAKE PLACE IN OUR LIVES.

The Nine Prayer Points of Completeness unfold in this sequence:

+ First, it is *God's* presence that impacts our *natural body.*

+ Next, it is *our spirit* that produces the *mental state* we operate in, which then determines our *emotional response* to things, which then dictates our *outlook on life.*

+ Our *outlook on life* will positively or negatively impact our *overall mood*, which will ultimately *define our character*, which will, in turn, *create our attitude* toward life and people.

+ Finally, it is our *attitude toward life and people* that determines how we handle the things we are faced with in this world, and how we respond to people.

---

1. "disposition," Dictionary.com, http://www.dictionary.com/browse/disposition (accessed April 25, 2017).

NINE PRAYER POINTS OF COMPLETENESS

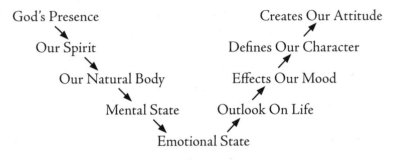

God's Presence   Creates Our Attitude

   Our Spirit   Defines Our Character

      Our Natural Body   Effects Our Mood

        Mental State   Outlook On Life

          Emotional State

© Dr. Jamie Pleasant Enterprises Inc.

Look at the Nine Prayer Points of Completeness more closely. Notice how we first expect an immediate change in our spirit. That is, we should know and feel that we have come into the presence of the almighty God. Second, our entire natural body should begin to calm down and settle into the awareness of almighty God—Father, Son, and Holy Spirit. Next, our mind should naturally relax and center itself, to make the spiritual reality of God accessible to us. As our mind engages in processing the spiritual things of God, so they can become a natural reality to us, our emotions are influenced by the state of our mind and reordered to a place of peace, trust, and tranquility.

Then, as our emotions are being shaped by the awareness of God's presence in the deepest parts of our soul, our outlook will begin to change in a more positive direction. This is when what is divine and hidden on the inside of us will now begin to be reflected in our actions—fully expressed in our facial demeanor and total disposition. Next, as our outlook on life changes, other people we come into contact with will begin to take notice and compliment us on our pleasing character and attitude. But let's not forget that our outward attitude is only a reflection of our inner spirit, which is being influenced by the presence of God.

> **OUR OUTWARD ATTITUDE IS ONLY A REFLECTION OF OUR INNER SPIRIT, WHICH IS BEING INFLUENCED BY THE PRESENCE OF GOD.**

The Nine Prayer Points of Completeness are the victory formation of the transfiguration that occurs through the process of prayer. This process produces a positive, prosperous outlook for us. Notice how the turning point in everything is hinged on our emotional state.

> **THE TURNING POINT OF CHANGE OCCURS AT THE EMOTIONAL STATE OF THE NINE PRAYER POINTS OF COMPLETENESS DURING THE PRAYER PROCESS.**

Also, we can't overlook the truth that nine is the number that represents the bearing of fruit in our lives. As you progress through this book, you should get ready to bear positive, uplifting fruit in your life. Get ready to bear the fruit of joy. Get ready to bear the fruit of peace. Get ready to bear the fruit of prosperity. Get ready to bear the fruit of confidence. Get ready to bear all the fruit of the Spirit, which are stated in Scripture:

> *But the fruit of the Spirit is love, joy, peace, patience, kindness, goodness, faithfulness, gentleness and self-control; against such things there is no law.*   (Galatians 5:22–23 NASB)

These things should manifest in us as we are in the act of praying. When we come out of prayer, the fruit of the Spirit should immediately be reflected in our daily lives.

Please pay special attention to what will happen at the end of our prayer experience when the fruit of the Spirit is manifested in our lives. The secret is found at the end of Galatians 5:23, which states: *"against such things there is no law."* How refreshing it is to know that when we give birth to the fruit of the Spirit during prayer, the natural laws of hurt, pain, disappointment, despair, or heartache can no longer have a negative effect in our lives. Those negative influences can't consume us because the fruit of the Spirit governs our being and protects all external circumstances and situations that are trying to get into our minds, hearts, and spirits.

> ONCE WE GIVE BIRTH TO THE FRUIT OF THE SPIRIT DURING PRAYER, THE NATURAL LAWS OF HURT, PAIN, DISAPPOINTMENT, DESPAIR, OR HEARTACHE CAN NO LONGER HAVE A NEGATIVE EFFECT IN OUR LIVES.

Our prayers should be fruitful in producing positive change in our lives regardless of what we are experiencing or going through at the present moment. Moreover, prayer should abolish every bitter root we are experiencing in our lives. Prayer should displace every doubt, hurt, pain, disappointment, and fear that may be plaguing us. Prayer should release the virtue of our heavenly Father through the Holy Spirit, which is reflected in our disposition when we pray, and still again after we pray.

> PRAYER SHOULD ABOLISH EVERY BITTER ROOT WE ARE EXPERIENCING IN OUR LIVES. PRAYER SHOULD DISPLACE EVERY DOUBT, HURT, PAIN, DISAPPOINTMENT, AND FEAR THAT MAY BE PLAGUING US.

Let us return to Luke 9:29:

As he was praying, the appearance of his face changed, and his clothes became as bright as a flash of lightning.

Notice, not only did His face or disposition change, but His clothes changed as well. The truth revealed here is that during prayer, not only are you experiencing a change, but everything that is attached to you is changing for the better also. Think about all the childhood doubt, rejection, disappointment, and hurt you still carry that refuses to let you go. Think about all the past shame and regret that continues to cling to you. How refreshing it is to know that as you are praying, all the evil and destructive things that plague you as you enter into prayer begin to change right before your eyes. They fall off of you in the middle of the transfiguring process of prayer.

What a blessing it is to know that we can take all our problems, doubts, and burdens to the Lord in prayer, release them, and then watch as they dwindle away as we are still praying. Prayer is the vehicle God uses to come to us and work through us.

> **PRAYER IS THE VEHICLE GOD USES TO COME TO US AND WORK THROUGH US.**

We should experience the miracle of change every time we pray. Change should not be something we hope happens *after* we pray. Prayer should produce change within us even before we say "Amen."

Try this exercise right now by beginning to pray. As you pray, hold your arms out with your palms up. Keep your eyes open and, as we did in chapter 1, envision heaven opening up to you. Next, sit and wait to hear God say something to you. He may speak in an audible voice, or He may whisper, quietly and intimately, within your spirit. Don't make the mistake of thinking that the voice you hear in your head is just you talking to yourself. More often than not, that is God speaking to you, through you. That's right, He speaks to you, through you.

GOD SPEAKS TO YOU, THROUGH YOU.

Center yourself and anticipate His voice. Once you hear from Him, write down what He says to you on the lines provided below. I promise that if you listen you are going to hear from God.

_____

_____

_____

_____

_____

_____

Next, write down what you felt in your body as you prayed with God.

_____

_____

_____

_____

_____

_____

You might have felt goose bumps at the base of your neck or a tingling sensation over your entire body. You might even have experienced chills running up and down your spine. Your hands may have become warm, as if mittens had been placed on them.

What a blessing it is to know that you have been in the presence of the almighty God Himself. Remember, when God shows up in your prayer time, you will feel Him, and you will experience change at that very moment.

Now that you have heard from God, felt His presence, and written down what He has said to you, write your own response to Him. It is important to write a response to everything that God says to you. It is God's way of knowing that you are taking this precious time that He spends with you very seriously.

_____

_____

_____

_____

_____

_____

CHAPTER 2: KEY POINT REVIEW

1. As we pray, change immediately begins to have a positive impact on our situations and circumstances.

2. Prayer has a profoundly positive impact on our spirits, minds, souls, and bodies.

3. God's presence, our spirit, our natural body, our mental state, our emotional state, our outlook on life, our mood, our character, and our attitude make up the Nine Prayer Points of Completeness that must unfold in order for positive change to take place in our lives.

4. Our outward attitude is only a reflection of our inner spirit being influenced by the presence of God.

5. The turning point of change occurs at the emotional state of the Nine Prayer Points of Completeness during the prayer process.

6. During prayer, once the fruit of the Spirit is produced in our lives, the natural laws of hurt, pain, and disappointment can no longer have negative effects in our lives.

7. Prayer should abolish every bitter root that we are experiencing in our lives.

8. Prayer is the vehicle God uses to come to us and work through us.

9. God speaks to you, through you.

SPIRITUAL EXERCISE

1. Write down the things you want God to reveal to you about being able to sense when change is taking place during your personal prayer time.

_____

_____

_____

_____

_____

_____

_____

2. Write down the key insights you learned in this chapter.

_____

_____

_____

_____

_____

_____

_____

3

OUR PRAYERS ARE ANSWERED BEFORE WE PRAY

Before they call I will answer;
while they are still speaking I will hear.
—Isaiah 65:24

Have you ever wondered how long it takes to get an answer from God when you pray?

Do you want to know what must happen in order to get an answer from God?

Do you want to know the proper things to do in order to hear from Him?

These questions will all be answered in this chapter. In fact, in all honesty, all three of these questions can easily be answered according to Isaiah 65:24:

Before they call I will answer; while they are still speaking I will hear.

The beauty of this Scripture is that it is not *after* prayer that we should anticipate an answer from God. It is not even *during* prayer that we should expect an answer from God. The truth revealed in Isaiah 65:24 shows us that before we pray, God has *already* answered all of our questions and responded to all of the requests we bring forward in prayer.

> **BEFORE WE PRAY, GOD HAS *ALREADY* ANSWERED ALL OF OUR QUESTIONS AND RESPONDED TO ALL OF THE REQUESTS WE BRING FORWARD IN PRAYER.**

God has prepared answers for our questions before we were even born, and prayer is how He unveiled these answers for us at specific times in our lives. Wow! What a beautiful revelation.

What an awesome truth it is to know that before we are born, God prepared answers for our questions, answers to help us in our present lives. This means that answers to all of the questions, doubts, concerns, and decisions that we are pondering are all floating around in spirit form, waiting to be revealed by God at the specific time He designed for us.

> **ANSWERS TO ALL OF THE QUESTIONS, DOUBTS, CONCERNS, AND DECISIONS THAT WE ARE PONDERING ARE ALL FLOATING AROUND IN SPIRIT FORM, WAITING TO BE REVEALED BY GOD AT THE SPECIFIC TIME HE DESIGNED FOR US.**

The key to transforming those answers in the spirit realm into an earthly form we can understand in the natural realm is only possible through the process of prayer. Prayer allows this transformation process to take place, in which spiritual truths and messages can be interpreted and understood.

PRAYER ALLOWS THIS TRANSFORMATION PROCESS TO TAKE PLACE, IN WHICH SPIRITUAL TRUTHS AND MESSAGES CAN BE INTERPRETED AND UNDERSTOOD.

A deeper look into Isaiah 65:24 shows us that the reason we feel a need to pray is because God has released an answer that He wants to birth in us for our present situation. It may simply be something that God wants to be revealed about our future, which has been purposed by Him.

THE REASON WE FEEL A NEED TO PRAY IS BECAUSE GOD HAS RELEASED AN ANSWER THAT HE WANTS TO BIRTH IN US FOR OUR PRESENT SITUATION.

What an interesting truth to know: When God has prepared an answer He wants us to hear and understand, He moves on us to begin the prayer process. We should note that prayer is not something *we* actually initiate. *God* does the initiation of the prayer process by moving on us with a desire to pray. Once we are moved to pray, or drawn to pray, God then moves in us to ask the right questions in prayer so that the answer can be clearly revealed to us.

WHEN GOD HAS PREPARED AN ANSWER HE WANTS US TO HEAR AND TO UNDERSTAND, HE MOVES ON US TO BEGIN THE PRAYER PROCESS.

Prayer is similar to the game show *Jeopardy*. If you have ever watched *Jeopardy*, you know that the contestants must choose categories based on different topics and different levels of rewards. The key to playing the game is that the contestants must respond to the answers in each category in the form of a question. Although all of the categories are random, the levels of difficulty for each answer within a category become more difficult as the reward amounts get larger.

For example, the category may be "American History." A contestant may choose American History for two hundred dollars. The two-hundred-dollar label is removed to reveal the answer: "He is the first African American to have a national holiday that is celebrated in the month of January." Notice that the answer is revealed when the contestant chooses that particular category. Next, the contestant must respond to the answer in the form of a question. The contestant then responds by asking, "Who is Martin Luther King Jr.?" The host, Alex Trebek, says, "That is the correct question," and the contestant is awarded two hundred dollars for knowing the correct question to the answer.

The answer was already there before the contestants showed up that day for the show. The answers were there waiting to be revealed. However, no one would know the correct question to ask until the appropriate answer was chosen and revealed. The contestants must be at the show on their scheduled day in order to unveil the answers that were prepared for them before they got there. The correct question lets you know that you have found the correct answer.

Now our walk with God is certainly not to be compared to a game show, but He operates in similar way for us. We are all contestants in a much more serious game called *Life*. God has prepared answers for us that are waiting to be revealed at a specified time. Those answers, though already prepared for us, can't be revealed until we call on them. We can't call on them unless we are invited to participate in the game.

On *Jeopardy*, screeners carefully evaluate the knowledge of potential contestants ahead of time to make sure they have a certain level of knowledge so that, as they become qualified, their chances of being successful on the show are good. If they are selected to compete, contestants can either accept the invitation to come on the show, or they can refuse to respond to the invitation. However, the initial invitation comes from the producers who own the show.

God invites us to participate on His "show," in which He prepares us to be successful once we participate in it. Accepting the invitation to participate is as easy as pausing in our busy lives and taking time to pray. This is the best way for us to succeed in experiencing an eternal and satisfying life right now!

> **PAUSING IN OUR BUSY LIVES AND TAKING TIME TO PRAY IS THE BEST WAY FOR US TO SUCCEED IN EXPERIENCING AN ETERNAL AND SATISFYING LIFE RIGHT NOW!**

Being obedient to God's invitation to pray is the same as participating on the game show *Jeopardy*. We must make the effort to pack our bags, make flight plans, and get to the show. In life, we must make time to make the trip in prayer in order to participate in what has already been prepared for us.

Notice, only when a contestant arrives at the correct TV studio and participates in the game can they be awarded the prize money. The point here is that we must be at the correct place at the correct time in order to receive the reward for knowing the right question to ask.

Now get this! Many people watch *Jeopardy* on their television sets each day and play along by asking the right questions to the revealed answers, but they don't get the prize money. Why? The money is not theirs because it was not their game. The game and rewards belong to the person who accepts the invitation to play the game and puts forth the effort to appear on the show.

Like the game of *Jeopardy*, prayer is the place we must go to ask the right questions. Our loving Master has already prepared the correct answers and is waiting to reveal them to us. Prayer is the place where we can choose the right category and receive a reward, but only if we know the right questions to ask. How beautiful it is to know that God has prequalified us to come to meet Him in a place of prayer, where we can be assured that we will be rewarded for asking the right questions. Wow! What a blessing we have in the miracle of prayer.

> **PRAYER IS THE PLACE WE MUST GO TO ASK THE RIGHT QUESTIONS. OUR LOVING MASTER HAS ALREADY PREPARED THE CORRECT ANSWERS AND IS WAITING TO REVEAL THEM TO US.**

God's answers are always in spiritual form, and they are constantly tugging at us. Remember, God initiates prayer. He invites us to pray. These spiritual answers keep tugging at us, and they refuse to go away until we enter into prayer. Once in prayer, as we begin to ask the correct questions, the answers are revealed in front of our eyes and we are rewarded for asking the correct questions. Our reward might be peace, a solution to a problem, wisdom for a clear decision that had to be made, healing for disease, the elimination of emotional or physical pain, and so much more. We will immediately feel better as we start hearing the answers. We then can move in the right direction, confident that we are infinitely better off than before the prayer process began.

Isaiah 65:24 states, *"Before they call I will answer; while they are still speaking I will hear."* While we are still speaking in prayer, God hears us.

Write a request to God below. Ask Him to begin to give you the ability to respond to His invitation of prayer time, a time in which answers can be revealed through you by asking the correct questions.

_____

_____

_____

_____

_____

_____

It may feel that you are making a request of God, and that He is answering in real time, but in truth, God already had an answer prepared for you. He was the One who moved on your heart to pray for His prepared, preordained answer. That may seem implausible but it is true. That is exactly what has taken place. The very fact that you are reading this book indicates that God has prepared you for such a time as this to allow His answers to be revealed to you.

The Hebrew word meaning "to hear" is *shama* (shaw-mah). *Shama* means "to give attention to." We must show God that we are attentive to His leadings, and He will respond by becoming attentive toward us. By asking the right questions, God is able to move us in the direction of His blessings, plans, and purposes that He preordained long before we were born.

> BY ASKING THE RIGHT QUESTIONS, GOD IS ABLE TO MOVE US IN THE DIRECTION OF HIS BLESSINGS, PLANS, AND PURPOSES THAT HE PREORDAINED LONG BEFORE WE WERE BORN.

Notice in Romans 10:17, the Scripture says,

Consequently, faith comes from hearing the message, and the message is heard through the word of Christ.

The key point here is to understand that we must speak the prophetic word of Christ first, then we are able to hear the answer and our faith is increased.

Speak the prophetic word of Christ.

↓

Our answer is received.

↓

Our faith is increased.

GETTING GOD TO ANSWER US IN PRAYER

Another way to look at this is to understand faith-producing prayer in its purest form is:

**If we ask God the correct questions,
revealed to us by Christ...**

↓

**God hears us and gives His full attention
to our question...**

↓

**Then He reveals answers that produce positive results
in our current situation.**

As we ask the correct questions that Christ has revealed to us, God gives attention to our questions with the intent on producing a positive outcome or faith in our lives. Once again, all of this takes place while we are asking the correct questions to God our Father.

A final point must be made here. It is the Holy Spirit who draws you to remember the correct questions that Christ Jesus has placed on your heart, which leads the Father to hear your prayers and act on your behalf. What a blessing to see the Father, Son, and Holy Spirit acting in concert to ensure our prayers are on point, on time, and in truth.

CHAPTER 3: KEY POINT REVIEW

1. Before we pray, God has *already* answered all of our questions and responded to all of the requests we bring forward in prayer.

2. Answers to all of the questions, doubts, concerns, and decisions that we are pondering are all floating around in spirit form, waiting to be revealed by God at the specific time He designed for us.

3. Prayer allows this transformation process to take place, in which spiritual truths and messages can be interpreted and understood.

4. The reason we feel a need to pray is because God has released an answer that He wants to birth in us for our present situation.

5. When God has prepared an answer He wants us to heart and to understand, He moves on us to begin the prayer process.

6. Pausing in our busy lives and taking time to pray is the best way for us to succeed in experiencing an eternal and satisfying life right now!

7. Prayer is the place we must go to ask the right questions. Our loving Master has already prepared the correct answers and is waiting to reveal them to us.

8. By asking the right questions, God is able to move us in the direction of His blessings, plans, and purposes that He preordained long before we were born.

SPIRITUAL EXERCISE

1. Write down the key things you want God to reveal to you about being able to sense when change is taking place during your personal prayer time.

_____

_____

_____

_____

_____

_____

2. Write down the key insights you learned in this chapter.

_____

_____

_____

_____

_____

_____

_____

4

WHEN WE ARE STILL, GOD IS ACTIVE

"Shout and be glad, Daughter Zion. For I am coming, and
I will live among you," declares the LORD. *"Many nations*
will be joined with the LORD *in that day and will become*
my people. I will live among you and you will know that the
LORD *Almighty has sent me to you. The* LORD *will inherit*
Judah as his portion in the holy land and will again choose
Jerusalem. **Be still** *before the* LORD, *all mankind, because he*
has roused himself from his holy dwelling."
—Zechariah 2:10–13

We often hear people say that we must be still and wait on the
Lord. Somehow, we take that to mean that God is always slow to
answer our prayers or to react to the things we are dealing with. In
truth, it is our ability to become still that allows Him to act swiftly.
It is our stillness in prayer that causes Him to move into our situations more quickly. That's right! We need to learn how to practice
stillness in life and in our prayer exercises.

This passage in Zechariah is a prophetic utterance in which
God takes a metaphoric measurement of Jerusalem. What is
revealed is not the physical dimensions of the existing city, but the

unlimited and glorious Jerusalem that is revealed as a Messianic prophecy of God's coming kingdom. What is suggested is that God's people need to be still so that God can move in their lives.

> **Be still** *before the* LORD, *all mankind, because he has roused himself from his holy dwelling.*

It is both a call to worship God and an order to allow Him to do His work. It is not a dismissive command to go away and shut up. It is an invitation to silently remain in His presence, "*before the* LORD." It is a promise that God is able to act while we are silent before Him. He is able to act on our behalf, immediately, and even simultaneously.

> ## GOD IS ABLE TO ACT WHILE WE ARE SILENT BEFORE HIM. HE IS ABLE TO ACT ON OUR BEHALF, IMMEDIATELY, AND EVEN SIMULTANEOUSLY.

To understand this better, we need to look at what the word "*still*" means. It is the Hebrew word *hacah* (ha-sa), which means "keep silence, hold your peace, hold your tongue, still, silence." As we approach prayer, there is a time when we should speak, but there should also be time when we should stop, quiet ourselves, and hold our peace. Approaching prayer with this mind-set will lead us to a place in prayer that will cause us to be still. In order to be still, we must stop worrying, stop doubting, and especially stop lying. We must also stop all of the busyness that distracts us from our prayer time with God. In fact, if we don't stop our *busyness* in prayer, God can't start His *business* of answering us. We must have an attitude of quietness and peacefulness before we are able to enter the deepest realm of prayer, which is to be still.

Let's be honest with ourselves. Too often in our busy lives, we stop to pray only when we are facing a crisis that places us in a state of uneasiness or stress. We often react to crisis by immediately praying for help or rescue. Please don't take this statement the wrong way. Whenever we are facing a crisis, we *should* enter into prayer to see what the Lord has to say. In times of stress and crisis, it is important to talk to God and let Him know what is immediately on our minds.

> **IF WE DON'T STOP OUR *BUSYNESS* IN PRAYER,**
> **GOD CAN'T START HIS *BUSINESS* OF ANSWERING US.**

What's important for us to realize is that we shouldn't rush into prayer with the wrong attitude and disposition. It is okay to pray when we are angry, but if possible, it's best for us to wait until we have settled down and calmed our emotions so we can ask God for proper things. We shouldn't enter into prayer in the heat of an argument with someone. We may become prone to ask God to curse or harm the other person. Not only is this not godly behavior, God won't move on such requests when we come to Him in that state of mind.

That is why practicing the truth of "stillness" is key for us to get God's attention to help us with whatever our crisis may be. Being still in prayer also allows Him to answer us and give us the proper instruction on how to handle any situation we are facing.

Looking deeper at this powerful word *"still,"* we find it means "to hold your peace." In order for God to move on your behalf, you must understand and know how to hold your peace. The key here is to not just get to a place of peace just before you pray, but to get peace and hold on to it. To hold on to peace means to receive it, feel it, and retain it. You must come into contact with peace and retain it in the midst of distractions during prayer. Your prayer only can be effective, and you will only be able to hear from God, after you attain and retain peace.

> ### TO HOLD ON TO PEACE MEANS TO RECEIVE IT, FEEL IT, AND RETAIN IT.

Peace can't be a fleeting or temporary thing. It must penetrate into the core of your very being. You must first receive the peace that can only come from God. Only then will you be able to retain peace with God. Once you are at peace with God, then you will also be at peace with yourself. It is only after you are at peace with yourself that you can approach Him in prayer and maintain that peace within your situation, until it too begins to change.

> ### YOU MUST FIRST RECEIVE THE PEACE THAT CAN ONLY COME FROM GOD.

STEPS FOR RECEIVING PEACE FROM GOD AND HOLDING ON TO IT UNTIL CHANGE COMES

You must get…

+ Peace from God
+ Peace with God
+ Peace within yourself
+ Peace in your situation, even if change hasn't come yet

Too many of us experience agitation, frustration, stress, and even depression within ourselves because we are not at peace with God. We are not at peace with God because we don't share our true feelings and concerns with Him. We seem to think that if we tell Him the truth, He will turn His ear away from us. So we never feel comfortable sharing the deepest truths about ourselves with God. Some of us even think that our honesty might cause God to disqualify us from being worthy to Him. We may also be afraid that as we expose our true selves to Him, He will punish us or shame us and make us feel bad. These fears couldn't be farther from the truth.

The truth is, when we share our deepest fears and feelings with God, our honesty shows Him that we trust Him. Then, we can obtain peace with God. Telling God the truth shows Him that we believe He is a God who forgives, and that we could never be perfect according to our own standards. Being honest shows God that we trust Him and need Him. Once we know that we can share our true selves with God in prayer, without fear of shame or punishment, we will find peace within ourselves as He moves to bring peace into our situations.

> ONCE WE KNOW THAT WE CAN SHARE OUR TRUE SELVES WITH GOD IN PRAYER, WITHOUT FEAR OF SHAME OR PUNISHMENT, WE WILL FIND PEACE WITHIN OURSELVES AS HE MOVES TO BRING PEACE INTO OUR SITUATIONS.

Pay special attention to the truth that He will bring peace to our crisis even if things haven't yet changed for the better. We may not see any positive change in our lives, but His peace will continue to hold us until change comes. We must see that the blessing in all of this is that we will stay in a peaceful state until our situation changes. This kind of peace is what I refer to as the "God-kind of peace." It is a level of peace that most people never experience or understand.

> GOD WILL BRING PEACE TO OUR CRISIS EVEN IF THINGS HAVEN'T YET CHANGED FOR THE BETTER.

This is the peace that surpasses all understanding in Philippians 4:7, which says,

And the peace of God, which transcends all understanding, will guard your hearts and your minds in Christ Jesus.

People who don't have a strong prayer life fail to understand how you can be at peace when your situation remains unchanged. They can't understand how you can remain faithful in praising God when your situation is still the same. They can't understand how you can be so joyful and calm in the middle of all the negative things that are happening to you. They can't and won't ever understand, because they have never experienced the "stillness" level in prayer that you have experienced, a level that not only allows you to find peace, but also to keep peace while you watch God act on your behalf. What a blessing to know this truth! Peace is there for you if you tap into it through prayer. We need to isolate ourselves from our external circumstances and concerns by learning how to enter into the stillness of prayer.

> **WE NEED TO ISOLATE OURSELVES FROM OUR EXTERNAL CIRCUMSTANCES AND CONCERNS BY LEARNING HOW TO ENTER INTO THE STILLNESS OF PRAYER.**

Take a moment and write a "confession prayer" to God. Tell Him that you trust Him with all your heart. Tell Him that you want to be more transparent and honest in your prayer life. Tell Him that you are glad to know that you will not be shamed or punished for things you've said or done in the past. Tell Him that you trust Him with your deepest concerns, and that you can't wait for Him to bring peace into your life, even before your situation changes.

_____

_____

_____

_____

_____

_____

To begin the learning process of entering into silence, try following these steps:

+ First, make sure you are in a quiet and isolated place where nothing or no one can disturb you.

+ Next, get into a comfortable position where you can maintain a certain posture that makes it easy for you to talk with the Lord. You may try sitting up straight in a chair. You may try reclining in a chair. You might even prefer standing. The point is to not choose a position that will become uncomfortable and shorten your time connecting with God. Choose a position in which you will be as comfortable as possible—without falling asleep!

+ After you have found a good position, breathe in and out.

+ Begin to focus on your breath.

+ As you inhale, think about the goodness of God and all He has done for you.

+ As you exhale, think about how much you love Him.

+ As you inhale, and think about the blessings you have received from God.

+ As you exhale, imagine your problem leaving you.

+ If your mind begins to wander, refocus your mind on your breath.

+ Inhale, picturing Him smiling at you and placing His hand on you—releasing a peace that you can now feel as it penetrates into your heart.

+ Exhale, releasing any stress, pain, worry, or other burden.

+ Inhale, and absorb a final precious moment of peace. Drink it in, feel it, and try to taste it.

+ Follow it up with one last long exhale.

Follow these steps twice. Write down how you feel after doing this.

_____

_____

_____

_____

_____

_____

_____

_____

_____

_____

_____

_____

Write down at least three things you inhaled in the exercise and three things you exhaled in the process.

I inhaled _____ the first time.

I exhaled _____ the first time.

I inhaled _____ the second time.

I exhaled _____ the second time.

I inhaled _____ the third time.

I exhaled _____ the third time.

Remember, the key is to make sure you are inhaling the goodness and blessings of God and exhaling the busyness and negative thoughts competing for your concentration in prayer. By continuing this practice, you will soon find yourself in the realm of stillness. Continue to anticipate and watch for God's presence. When you reach a point in the inhaling and exhaling exercise that you can are aware of God's presence and feel connected with Him, you have reached the *first level of stillness*. When your thoughts become totally peaceful and heavenly, you have reached the *second level of stillness*. When you become aware only of the presence of God and nothing or no one else, you have reached the *third level of stillness*. Once you have achieved the third level of stillness, you are now ready to hear Him speak, and to watch Him take action on your behalf. This is the *fourth level of stillness*.

Remember, stillness is the key to becoming one with God, an essential step toward allowing Him to begin to act on your behalf to change both you and your situation. Stillness allows action to be taken by God. A special word of caution must be given here: we can't go to the highest level of stillness until we have first achieved all of the lower levels of stillness.

STILLNESS IS THE KEY TO BECOMING ONE WITH GOD, AN ESSENTIAL STEP TOWARD ALLOWING HIM TO BEGIN TO ACT ON YOUR BEHALF TO CHANGE BOTH YOU AND YOUR SITUATION.

LEVELS OF STILLNESS

You clearly
hear from God.

You become aware only of
the presence of God.

Your thoughts become totally
peaceful and heavenly.

You can feel God, and totally feel
connected with Him.

CHAPTER 4: KEY POINT REVIEW

1. God is able to act while we are silent before Him. He is able to act on our behalf, immediately, and even simultaneously.

2. If we don't stop our *busyness* in prayer, God can't start His *business* of answering us.

3. To hold on to peace means to receive it, feel it, and retain it.

4. You must first receive the peace that can only come from God.

5. When we share our deepest feelings with God, our honesty shows Him we trust Him. Then, we can get peace with God.

6. He will bring peace to our crisis even if things haven't changed for the better.

7. Once we know that we can share our true selves with God in prayer, without fear of shame or punishment, we will find peace within ourselves as He moves to bring peace into our situations.

8. God will bring peace to our crisis even if things haven't yet changed for the better.

9. We need to isolate ourselves from our external circumstances and concerns by learning how to enter into the stillness of prayer.

10. Stillness is the key to becoming one with God, an essential step toward allowing Him to begin to act on your behalf to change both you and your situation.

11. We can't go to the highest level of stillness until we have first achieved all of the lower levels of stillness.

SPIRITUAL EXERCISE

1. Write down the things you want God to reveal to you about being able to sense when change is taking place during your personal prayer time.

_____

_____

_____

_____

_____

_____

_____

2. Write down any insights you learned in this chapter.

_____

_____

_____

_____

_____

_____

_____

5

PRAYING FROM YOUR HEART

Hannah was praying in her heart, and her lips were moving but her voice was not heard. Eli thought she was drunk and said to her, "How long are you going to stay drunk?"
—1 Samuel 1:13–14

When we think about praying the perfect prayer, we may imagine all of the ways we've heard others pray. We may listen to others and settle on using their style and words in prayer as our own. Some of us have picked certain prayers from the Bible as "the perfect prayer." Others may rely on the latest Christian authors to craft and they make these prayers their own. This chapter will challenge your thinking on what is the "perfect prayer."

Let's look at 1 Samuel 1:13–16:

Hannah was praying in her heart, and her lips were moving but her voice was not heard. Eli thought she was drunk and said to her, "How long are you going to stay drunk? Put away your wine." "Not so, my lord," Hannah replied, "I am a woman who is deeply troubled. I have not been drinking wine or beer; I was pouring out my soul to the Lord. Do not take your servant for a wicked woman; I have been praying here out of my great anguish and grief."

Look at the richness of these Scriptures! There is so much here to learn and embrace. This chapter can only begin to show us the best prayer we can offer to God every time we come humbly to His throne of greatness. It can only begin the process and lay the foundation. The rest is up to us in our quest to come to God uniquely, honestly, openly, and totally connected to Him in prayer. Once we study the truths in this chapter and meditate on 1 Samuel 1:13–16, we should be able to begin to pray our best prayers to God.

Notice that verse 13 shows us that Hannah was praying in her heart. She comes to God in the purest way she knows—not with her head or with methods she learned at the temple, and not with words she heard someone else pray. She came to God in prayer and opened her heart to Him. Too many of us approach prayer by coming to God based on what we have heard others pray. We close our eyes, clasp our hands, and sit up straight. We may use formal words: "Oh Great High God Jehovah. You are the Lord of Lords and Master of all things. How great is Your name and greatness! You are the one who makes the sun shine in the morning. You are the one who makes the moon shine at night. You are the one who makes the grass green and the flowers bloom." On the other hand, we may get too comfortable and confident in His presence, throwing in lines like this: "You are the only God that can make a brown cow eat green grass to produce white milk."

> **TOO MANY OF US APPROACH PRAYER BY COMING TO GOD BASED ON WHAT WE HAVE HEARD OTHERS PRAY.**

We go on and on and on and on. Then we wonder why, after all of our eloquent and flamboyant salutations, we still can't feel God presence or hear from Him. We wonder what else we could have done to move on God's heart and get Him to answer us. Matthew 6:7–8 says:

> And when you pray, do not keep on babbling like pagans, for they think they will be heard because of their many words. Do not be like them, for your Father knows what you need before you ask him.

We shouldn't continue babbling on and on in our prayers. Matthew makes it clear that praying this way is unnecessary with God. Most people pray like this to God because they are trying to convince themselves that they are in a right relationship with Him. Some people pray like this because they are trying to convince God that they have reached a certain level of importance and spirituality. Others pray this way because they are using flattery and false humility—fooling themselves into thinking that God can't see through their tricks. The word *"babbling"* comes from the Greek word *battalogeō*, which means "vain repetitions." In other words, the effort invested in long meaningless flattery and charm to God will not produce any more of a blessing in our lives at all.

> ## THE EFFORT INVESTED IN LONG MEANINGLESS FLATTERY AND CHARM TO GOD WILL NOT PRODUCE ANY MORE OF A BLESSING IN OUR LIVES AT ALL.

In fact, Matthew 6:7–8 goes on further to say that God doesn't want us to be like pagans, or to pray like them, because it is simply a waste of time. God already knows what we want and need before we ask Him. We should come to prayer the following way. We should pray in time, pray in truth, and pray on point.

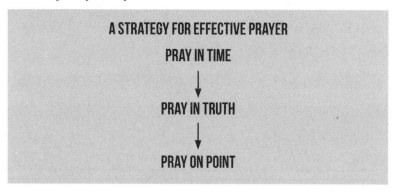

IN TIME

Every time we come to the part in prayer in which we talk or initiate the conversation with God, we should pray in time. This means we are aware that God has allowed a certain window of time for us to connect with Him uniquely. Don't waste time with words that are empty and not full of power. These words cannot connect with God. And God cannot meet the needs He already knows we have if we pray a useless prayer to Him.

IN TRUTH

We then must pray in truth. In other words, we must pray like Hannah prayed. She simply opened her heart and prayed from within with all her might. She prayed from within herself, and with all the truth about herself. She wanted her truth to touch God's truth. God's truth is what He knows we should pray before we begin to pray, and what He expects us to pray knowing who we are.

WE SHOULD PRAY FROM WITHIN OURSELVES, AND WITH ALL THE
TRUTH ABOUT OURSELVES.

When our truth can touch God's truth, a connection is made and blessings flow from heaven. Touching our truth with God's truth is simply allowing our heart to touch God's heart. So, we don't have to waste a lot of time with empty words to God. If we speak to God in truth, the connection is quickly made and heaven opens.

> **IF WE SPEAK TO GOD IN TRUTH, THE CONNECTION IS QUICKLY MADE AND HEAVEN OPENS.**

ON POINT

Finally, once we are in truth, then we must pray on point. Praying on point means we must know the right words to pray to God. In other words, we must know the precise truth to speak to God about. Here is where a lot of people miss so much of the effectiveness of prayer. We must pray on point, without jumping and skipping around with words in a wild attempt at reaching God's heart. We can't just keep going on and on with our "word salad" in some mad attempt to feel something that resembles God's anointing or His presence. So many people babble on in prayer and miss the chance to prayer on point in such a way that they see heaven open.

Praying on point is not a very difficult thing to do, but it does take some time and mental focus. Once you are comfortable with it, praying on point will come quickly, but in the beginning, it will require effort for you to quiet your soul. Go before God in a quiet, secluded place. Before praying, take a few moments to reject any anti-God thoughts, to eliminate any external distractions, and to reject any negative influences that may be trying to affect you. By doing this, you will become more centered and still, and your heart will begin to actually engage with the heart of God. As you continue in this, your heart will begin to open up and you will be able to speak *truth* to God. It is the truth that you speak from your heart that connects with the truth of God. Prayer is not meant for small talk that simply takes up time. Prayer time is meant for an exchange of truth between you and Your Creator—the One who knows you best. Once your truth is spoken, all you have to do is wait and watch for heaven to open. Your heart reaching God's heart, and your truth reaching God's truth, opens up heaven just as a key unlocks a door.

Take a moment to practice this effective three-step strategy: praying in time, praying in truth, and praying on point. When you are done, write down what you experienced during this exercise.

_____

_____

_____

_____

_____

_____

Again, prayer is not a place to come and waste valuable time convincing, pleading, and politicking about what we want God to do for us. Prayer is also not the place where we come to try to get His attention about something we need because we feel He is so busy doing other things that He is not aware of that need. No! Prayer is the place where we can come and connect with Him for more than just having our needs met. We should expect our needs to be exceeded by God.

PRAYER IS THE PLACE WHERE WE CAN COME AND CONNECT WITH HIM FOR MORE THAN JUST HAVING OUR NEEDS MET.

The truth of this is found in Ephesians 3:20:

Now to him who is able to do immeasurably more than all we ask or imagine, according to his power that is at work within us....

How wonderful it is to know that God will exceed all of our needs. Here is a better way to look at this Scripture. When we connect with God in time, in truth, and on point, all the divine supply we need is released by God through prayer. Prayer is the way in which God releases His supply to meet our needs. He already knows what we need and when our needs should be met.

Now let's build on that with what we have learned in the previous chapters. When we feel a tugging in our hearts to go to God in prayer, it means that the time has come for Him to release His supply to us in our time of need. He is drawing us to Him.

As we center and quiet ourselves by exhaling everything that is not of God and inhaling everything that is of God, we open ourselves up, speak our deepest truth, and then we watch as heaven opens up and God releases our supply. We know that there is a specific period of time that heaven opens and the supply God is released to us. We should watch closely and wait until we see our supply from God come to us.

> **WE KNOW THAT THERE IS A SPECIFIC PERIOD OF TIME THAT HEAVEN OPENS AND THE SUPPLY FROM GOD IS RELEASED TO US.**

Look again at 1 Samuel 1:13. It says, *"Hannah was praying in her heart."* We must focus again on her intention about this prayer. She was praying in her heart. She wasn't trying to be cute with God. She wasn't trying to impress Him or flatter Him. She simply had reached a point in her life in which she wanted to see a change in her situation. She felt hurt, defeated, and full of doubt. She wanted a baby.

All of the other women had children. Why couldn't Hannah have a child? How embarrassed it must have been for her to go into town and to worship knowing that people were talking about her inability to conceive. In those days, barrenness was one of the worst things that could happen to a woman. Not being able to have children was considered a curse and a sign of personal weakness. She had tried so many times to get pregnant. She had been told by everyone that she would never have any children. She found herself isolated, rejected by society, and full of questions for God.

There it is! She became full of many questions for God. All of a sudden, she found herself drawn to prayer. Notice, she was not praying at home. She was not calling every prayer line on Christian television. She was not asking everyone in the church to pray and lay hands on her and enter into agreement that she would get pregnant. No! She was drawn to prayer. That drawing was so strong that she found herself at the place of worship in front of the High Priest Eli.

She had to leave her place of doubt, trouble, and fear, and go where she felt the tugging lead her of her heart. Once she got there, she didn't care what anyone else said about her. She didn't care how anyone might look at her. She didn't even care if she appeared to be insane or drunk. All she knew was that she was drawn to prayer. The power to pray was so strong on her that she had to get to a place where she could pour out her heart—her truth—to God. She let Him know what was on her mind, and then she waited to see heaven open.

What a blessing! She opened up her heart to God and He opened up His heart to her. As a result, her womb was opened up. Yes! Her womb was opened as heaven was opened and as God's heart was opened. All of this happened because she first opened up her heart in truth to God.

Let this be a lesson and example for all of us. If we really want to see the hand of God in our lives, we must make the effort to not be afraid to become truthful with Him whenever He chooses us to come to prayer in truth.

We should also not overlook the importance of our local church, which God has called us to be a part of. Hannah had to get up, dress up, and go up to her local place of worship and lay everything open to God, and to everyone else who was able to see everything about her. It was her obedience to being drawn by the hand of God in prayer that brought her healing that day. Hannah walked in that place of worship determined not to leave the way she came in. She came in empty; she left full. She came in weak; she left with power. She came in hurt; she left with joy.

What a powerful resource we have when we accept the invitation of God for prayer. Just like the *Jeopardy* example in chapter 3, we must accept the invitation to the game, where the answers have already been prepared for us. All that is left for us to do is bring our questions to God in prayer, and the answers are revealed to us every time as heaven opens up.

CHAPTER 5: KEY POINT REVIEW

1. Too many of us approach prayer by coming to God based on what we have heard others pray.

2. We shouldn't continue babbling on and on in our prayers.

3. We should pray in time, pray in truth, and pray on point.

4. We should pray from within ourselves, and with all the truth about ourselves.

5. Our truth should touch God's truth.

6. If we speak to God in truth, the connection is quickly made and heaven opens.

7. Prayer is the place where we can come and connect with Him for more than just having are needs met.

8. We know that there is a specific period of time that heaven opens and the supply from God is released to us.

9. All that is left for us to do is bring our questions to God in prayer, and the answers are revealed to us every time as heaven opens up.

SPIRITUAL EXERCISE

1. Write down the things you want God to reveal to you about being able to sense when change is taking place during your personal prayer time.

_____

_____

_____

_____

_____

_____

_____

2. Write down any insights you learned in this chapter.

_____

_____

_____

_____

_____

_____

_____

6

A PRAYER THAT
ONLY GOD CAN HEAR

*...and her lips were moving but her voice was not heard. Eli
thought she was drunk and said to her, "How long will you
keep on getting drunk? Put away your wine."*
—1 Samuel 1:13–14

In the previous chapter, we learned about Hannah's perfect prayer
to God. There is much more we can gain from Hannah's prayer.

Pay close attention to this Scripture and you will discover
another prayer secret. The secret is that there is a realm or level of
prayer that we can reach that will allow us to go beyond what we
ourselves and others can hear and understand as we pray. In other
words, there is a point in prayer in which we will be so in tune with
the Holy Spirit that we will look like we are doing natural, physical things, when, in fact, we have transitioned into a supernatural
realm. Watch this!

Hannah was so focused and involved in her prayer that Eli, the
High Priest watched her move her lips but he couldn't hear anything. He even got frustrated at seeing her move her lips while no
sound was coming out of her mouth. He assumed she was drunk,
and he sharply rebuked her to stop drinking so much wine.

This is one of the most beautiful things that can happen in prayer. Notice that her lips moved, but the words she spoke couldn't be heard. Think about that. What could be the reason that her lips moved but the words couldn't be heard? Well, it is one of the biggest blessings God can provide for us in prayer. It is called intercession. That's right! This is a great example of the intercessory ministry of the Holy Spirit. Romans 8:26–27 says,

> *In the same way, the Spirit helps us in our weakness. We do not know what we ought to pray for, but the Spirit himself intercedes for us through wordless groans. And he who searches our hearts knows the mind of the Spirit, because the Spirit intercedes for God's people in accordance with the will of God.*

Yes! The Holy Spirit intercedes for us when we don't know what to say in our prayers. It is when we don't know what to say in prayer that we can get lost and mess up our prayers. When our prayers are messed up, they aren't effective in getting God's attention.

THE HOLY SPIRIT INTERCEDES FOR US WHEN WE DON'T KNOW WHAT TO SAY IN OUR PRAYERS.

Let's look at the meaning of the word *intercede*. It has a three-pronged meaning that must be dealt with in its entirety to completely understand the great work of the Holy Spirit. The word *intercede* means to:

a. to act or interpose in behalf of someone in difficulty or trouble, as by pleading or petition;

b. to attempt to reconcile differences between two people or groups; mediate

Please note that there is a progressive unfolding of the word *intercede*. First, the Holy Spirit will interpose (place Himself between us and the Father) during prayer to listen to both sides to see what is being said. Next, the Holy Spirit will mediate to reconcile our differences in order to bring our prayers in line with God's will. Only then will our prayers be heard and answered by God.

> ## THE HOLY SPIRIT WILL MEDIATE TO RECONCILE OUR DIFFERENCES IN ORDER TO BRING OUR PRAYERS IN LINE WITH GOD'S WILL.

THE HOLY SPIRIT INTERCEDES FOR US IN PRAYER BY:

1. Intervening between us and the Father.

2. Listening to both sides to see what is being said.

3. Bringing our prayers in line with God's will, so that our prayers are heard and answered by God only.

What a blessing that is! Now, let's go back to Hannah in 1 Samuel 1:13, where it says, *"and her lips were moving but her voice was not heard."* Pay close attention to this. Her lips were moving but the words couldn't be heard by Eli the priest. Why? She was no longer speaking in prayer through her flesh. She was praying from her heart with the assistance of the Holy Spirit. She had to be praying with the assistance of the Holy Spirit. She had come to the temple many times before and prayed but no answer had ever come to her. Perhaps she had been angry and bitter that she had said the wrong things in prayer. Maybe she didn't know the correct things to say. Maybe she just was going through the motions and thought that merely praying anything was good enough.

However, this time, something great happened to her when she came to the temple to pray. She encountered a realm of prayer in which the Holy Spirit stepped in and made her prayer perfect for God's purpose. The Holy Spirit first looked at what Christ had placed in her heart to say. Next, when He saw that she was ready to pray from her heart to God's heart, He had to make sure that her words would not fall on the wrong ears and delay God's reply. The Holy Spirit then had to make sure that anyone eavesdropping on her prayers would not bring harm or ridicule to her. Thus, her words were not heard by anyone but God the Father.

THE HOLY SPIRIT STEPS IN AND MAKES OUR PRAYER PERFECT FOR GOD'S PURPOSE.

As she prayed, the Holy Spirit then made sure her words were shaped in the will of God the Father. As a result, her words reached heaven and it opened up her womb. What great news it is to know that the Holy Spirit will take our prayers and tune them in to a frequency so that only God can hear what is in our heart. Eli the Priest couldn't even hear or understand her words because they were words from her heart to God and no one else.

Finally, through the guidance of the Holy Spirit, her prayers reached God, as Eli told her that what she had prayed for was going to come to pass. How interesting it is that Eli never heard what she was saying, but God moved on his heart to tell her that the prayer she had offered to God had been answered. Notice the beauty of this. God moved in her heart to speak from her heart. She then spoke from her heart to God's heart. Next, God moved on Eli's heart to speak His answer to her. Did you see the blessing in that? Hannah prayed from her heart, but the priest had to deliver the answer. Sometimes, we can pray in our hearts with all our might and still not be able to hear what God is saying. The assurance we have of a heart-felt prayer is that sometimes, God will send an answer to our prayers through someone else who He chooses.

SOMETIMES, GOD WILL SEND AN ANSWER TO OUR PRAYERS THROUGH SOMEONE ELSE.

Never forget the importance of a pastor in your life. That is why church attendance is so important, even today, when we have the Holy Spirit permanently in our lives. After all the interceding the Holy Spirit will do for us, He will still move on the hearts of others, including pastors, to relay God's answer to us. He never stops working until we get an answer.

When we go to church and a Holy Spirit-anointed pastor starts talking, everything he says sounds as though it is intended just for us. You will find yourself saying things like, "I thought he was only talking to me" or "That word was just what I needed." You may wonder if the pastor has a microphone in your house. You will ask, "How did he know that I was dealing with that?" You will recognize that a particular section of your pastor's sermon was targeted directly to our hearts. You'll say, "That message spoke to my heart." Guess what? It did. It was an answer to a prayer that came from your heart and reached God's heart. Now, you are receiving the blessing of God's answer to your prayers through your pastor's words. Even in a time when people think the importance of a pastor is small, or they think that as long as they have Christ, they have everything they need, we must be mindful of the fact that the work and ministry of the Holy Spirit was given by Christ to make sure that all believers can pray a perfect prayer that lines up with the will of God.

> **THE WORK AND MINISTRY OF THE HOLY SPIRIT WAS GIVEN BY CHRIST TO MAKE SURE THAT ALL BELIEVERS CAN PRAY A PERFECT PRAYER THAT LINES UP WITH THE WILL OF GOD.**

Look at John 16:7:

But very truly I tell you, it is for your good that I am going away. Unless I go away, the Advocate will not come to you; but if I go, I will send him to you.

Now watch what Christ Jesus says about the blessing we will have when the Holy Spirit comes into our lives to help us in prayer. John 16:13–15 says,

> But when he, the Spirit of truth, comes, he will guide you into all truth. He will not speak on his own; he will speak only what he hears, and he will tell you what is yet to come. He will glorify me because it is from me that he will receive what he will make known to you. All that belongs to the Father is mine. That is why I said the Spirit will receive from me what he will make known to you.

Yes! The Holy Spirit has a job. His main job is to make known to us whatever Christ wants us to hear, and to receive whatever the Father has ordained for us to know. Christ says the answer that the Father gives us will be made known to us in whatever fashion or form He chooses. However, the Holy Spirit has to make it happen. This is His major responsibility on this earth. So, if He has to speak through a pastor to get the message to us, He will. If He has to speak through a prophet to get the message to us, He will. Even if He has to speak through a donkey to get the message to us, He will. The message will get to us.

> **THE HOLY SPIRIT'S MAIN JOB IS TO MAKE KNOWN TO US WHATEVER CHRIST WANTS US TO HEAR, AND TO RECEIVE WHATEVER THE FATHER HAS ORDAINED FOR US TO KNOW.**

Examine 2 Peter 2:15–16:

> They have left the straight way and wandered off to follow the way of Balaam son of Bezer, who loved the wages of wickedness. But he was rebuked for his wrongdoing by a donkey—an animal without speech—who spoke with a human voice and restrained the prophet's madness.

Yes! In order for His will to be done, God used the Holy Spirit to speak through a donkey to save His prophet. If God can speak through a donkey, He can speak through a pastor, prophet, or any person. That's how much He loves us. And, that's how much we must be open to hearing an answer from God's heart. What a blessing it is to know that when it is time for God's purpose to be unfolded in our lives, the Holy Spirit will stand in the gap for us. He will speak for us and through us so that what is in our hearts is correctly expressed to the Father.

> **WHAT A BLESSING IT IS TO KNOW THAT WHEN IT IS TIME FOR GOD'S PURPOSE TO BE UNFOLDED IN OUR LIVES, THE HOLY SPIRIT WILL STAND IN THE GAP FOR US. HE WILL SPEAK FOR US AND THROUGH US SO THAT WHAT IS IN OUR HEARTS IS CORRECTLY EXPRESSED TO THE FATHER.**

As you pray to God, ask the Holy Spirit to intercede with you and for you. Pray from your heart without speaking any words out of your mouth and record what you experience below.

_____

_____

_____

_____

_____

_____

Silent prayer keeps us focused on the truthfulness in our hearts that is trying to express itself externally, without us messing it up. That's right! There are times when we can and will mess up a perfect prayer, causing us to miss out on God's ability to act according to His will concerning a situation or circumstance in our lives. In other words, sometimes our words get in the way of the Holy Spirit-truth that is trying to come out of us. In such times, we need help to ensure we are making a perfect prayer that will unlock God's answers and purpose in our lives.

> SILENT PRAYER KEEPS US FOCUSED ON THE TRUTHFULNESS IN OUR HEARTS THAT IS TRYING TO EXPRESS ITSELF EXTERNALLY, WITHOUT US MESSING IT UP.

To be honest, sometimes, when we don't know what to say, we talk ourselves out of a blessing from God. We may even talk ourselves into a mess based on our inability to speak the right things in prayer.

Notice again Romans 8:26:

In the same way, the Spirit helps us in our weakness. We do not know what we ought to pray for, but the Spirit himself intercedes for us through wordless groans.

The Holy Spirit will help us in our areas of weakness concerning our inability sometimes to speak a perfect prayer. The Holy Spirit will move from within us and activate the truth that Christ has placed in us. The Holy Spirit will make sure that our words are truly and correctly expressed to the Father.

Let's look at 1 Samuel 1:15–16 once more:

"Not so, my lord," Hannah replied, "I am a woman who is deeply troubled. I have not been drinking wine or beer; I was pouring out my soul to the LORD. Do not take your servant for a wicked woman; I have been praying here out of my great anguish and grief."

Hannah admits that she is at a very weak point in her life. She is deeply troubled and praying out of great anguish and grief. Anyone can easily recognize that she needs help, comfort, and guidance.

> ## IT IS WHEN WE APPROACH PRAYER ADMITTING TO GOD THAT WE ARE WEAK, HE SENDS THE HOLY SPIRIT TO HELP US.

Thank God the Holy Spirit moved in Hannah's life. And He will move in our lives in the same way as well. In fact, it was when she came to the realization that she was weak, tired, and not strong enough to bring change in her life that the Holy Spirit was able to move on her and help her in prayer. Our approach should be the same. We need to know when to admit to God that we are weak in mind, heart, and spirit about the things of life. It is when we take this humble approach to God that He sends the Holy Spirit to help us.

> ## IT IS WHEN WE TAKE THIS HUMBLE APPROACH TO GOD THAT HE SENDS THE HOLY SPIRIT TO HELP US.

When it comes to prayer, we should not be afraid to admit we are weak. It is in our admission of weakness that we will find strength in the Holy Spirit. Even the apostle Paul experienced this:

> *But he said to me, "My grace is sufficient for you, for my power is made perfect in weakness." Therefore I [Paul] will boast all the more gladly about my weaknesses, so that Christ's power may rest on me.*   (2 Corinthians 12:9)

Paul learned a valuable lesson in humility when it comes to praying to God. He learned that you must not be afraid to express your frustration, pain, and grief to the Father when you pray. Are you frustrated about some things in life? Are you experiencing pain in your heart about something that happened to you? Are you grieving over something or someone you recently lost? If so, admit your true feelings to Him. Then watch and see if His power won't come and rest on you.

Take a moment right now to write out a prayer about the things you are frustrated about, hurting from, or grieving over.

_____

_____

_____

_____

_____

_____

CHAPTER 6: KEY POINT REVIEW

1. The Holy Spirit intercedes for us when we don't know what to say in our prayers.

2. The Holy Spirit will mediate to reconcile our differences in order to bring our prayers in line with God's will.

3. The Holy Spirit steps in and makes our prayer perfect for God's purpose.

4. Sometimes, God will send an answer to our prayers through someone else.

5. The work and ministry of the Holy Spirit was given by Christ to make sure that all believers can pray a perfect prayer that lines up with the will of God.

6. The Holy Spirit's main job is to make known to us whatever Christ wants us to hear, and to receive whatever the Father has ordained for us to know.

7. What a blessing it is to know that when it is time for God's purpose to be unfolded in our lives, the Holy Spirit will stand in the gap for us. He will speak for us and through us so that what is in our hearts is correctly expressed to the Father.

8. Silent prayer keeps us focused on the truthfulness in our hearts that is trying to express itself externally, without us messing it up.

9. It is when we take this humble approach to God that He sends the Holy Spirit to help us.

SPIRITUAL EXERCISE

1. Write down the things you want God to reveal to you about being able to sense when change is taking place during your personal prayer time.

_____

_____

_____

_____

_____

_____

2. Write down any insights you learned in this chapter.

_____

_____

_____

_____

_____

_____

_____

7

GOD WILL SPEAK TO YOU, THROUGH YOU

The word of the LORD came to me, saying....
—Jeremiah 1:4

As children of God, we all believe in the power of prayer. There is no doubt that when we enter into prayer we have an assurance that God will hear the words we speak to Him. However, when it comes to hearing a reply from Him, many of us are not as confident about when, how, and where it will come. Practically speaking, this unsure approach to prayer is not an effective strategy.

If your approach to prayer involves first talking to God and then waiting to hear from Him, you need to realize that this is not the way prayer has been designed. God designed prayer to be an open line of communication between Him and us. This open line can be initiated on either end. The point is to understand that prayer is *the* method God uses to communicate whatever He wants, whenever He wants. Prayer is God's unique way of being involved in our lives. It is the chief way in which He communicates His will to us. Because of this, we should expect Him to lead us into prayer often.

> **PRAYER IS *THE* METHOD GOD USES TO COMMUNICATE WHATEVER HE WANTS, WHENEVER HE WANTS.**

If you look at Scripture carefully, you discover that God initiated most of the prayers that mankind encountered. For example, look at Jeremiah 1:4:

The word of the Lord came to me, saying….

Notice that Jeremiah didn't approach God; God approached Jeremiah. But Jeremiah recognized that it was the Word of the Lord that he was hearing. Not only did Jeremiah recognize that it was the *word* of the Lord, he also knew it was the *voice* of the Lord, because he stated so. He made it clear that the word not only came to him, but it *"came…saying."* This is the most powerful part.

It was not a rhetorical word. It was not a reported word. It was a real time conversation with God where he could understand audibly what God was saying. Here we can see clearly the Word of the Lord came to him speaking. That's right! The Word of the Lord came to him speaking truth, purpose, and power. God's Word came to him so that he would know how God was going to use him in the future.

There are many other examples in the Bible that demonstrate how God initiated prayer with those He wanted to use to execute His will. We should stay alert and watchful of God to speak to us and through us with truth, purpose, and power.

> **WE SHOULD STAY ALERT AND WATCHFUL OF GOD TO SPEAK TO US AND THROUGH US WITH TRUTH, PURPOSE, AND POWER.**

Some of the questions people ask themselves in regards to understanding prayer are:

+ How do I recognize the voice of God?

+ How will I know God is answering me?

+ How can I be sure God is speaking to me?

+ How can I be confident that God is speaking to me, and I am not talking to myself?

+ How can I recognize the voice of God speaking to me the way Jeremiah did?

The answers to these questions are found in the fact that God can speak to us in many ways, but we must recognize when, how, where, and through whom He may choose to speak.

The first and most important way we must recognize that He may choose to speak is through us. He desires to speak to us by speaking through us. We should not become uneasy about the fact that God prefers to speak directly through us as He is speaking directly to us. This is really the fastest, easiest, and purest way He can speak to us. It is a direct line between us and Him where no one can tamper with the truthfulness of what He wants us to hear from Him.

The truth that we must accept here is that God speaks very often through us in order to speak to us. However, most of us will confuse this with thinking that we are just talking to ourselves. We may think that we are just hearing our own voice in our heads. We may make the mistake of missing Him speak to us by saying things like, "something told me to," or "something said to me." We must make sure we don't miss His voice by thinking something or someone told us something in our heads when it was really God's voice we heard.

Take a moment and think about the time when you approached an intersection. You pushed the accelerator down to the floor to speed through the traffic light. Then suddenly, you heard a voice in your head say, "Don't go through that light!" "Slow down and stop!" You stopped and another car coming from the opposite side of the intersection sped through the light. If you had not stopped, you would have been in an accident. You took a deep breath and said, "Something told me not to go through that light!" I am here to tell you that it was not "something" that spoke to you. It wasn't even "someone" who spoke to you. It was God that spoke through you to you! Yes! God had to get that message to you very quickly or there would have been devastating results at that intersection you were about to cross. He spoke quickly and directly through you to protect you. There was not enough time for someone else to tell you to slow down. It would have been too late. There had to be an immediate line of communication where there was no doubt on your part that God was speaking. God used the Holy Spirit to speak on His behalf in the form of your own voice to save you from being in an accident.

> **GOD WILL USE THE HOLY SPIRIT TO SPEAK ON HIS BEHALF IN THE FORM OF YOUR OWN VOICE.**

Scripture supports this truth in 2 Samuel 23:2:

The Spirit of the Lord spoke through me; his word was on my tongue.

Do you see it? Samuel shows us that the Lord spoke through David and instructed him on what to say. In other words, David is speaking in his own voice, but it is God who is directing what he says. We must stop saying, "something told me." We must now say, "The Holy Spirit told me," or "God told me."

Let's take another look at Psalm 45:1:

My heart is stirred by a noble theme as I recite my verses for the king; my tongue is the pen of a skillful writer.

Here, David shows us that his tongue was being directed by the mouth of God. In other words, whatever God instructed his tongue to say, David said. Our tongues should be under the authority of God, and available to be used by Him, however He wants to use them. This is what happens when someone prophesies to us. Even though they are speaking in their own voice, it is God speaking through them to us.

> **YOU WILL BEGIN TO EXPERIENCE A PEACEFUL AND GODLY PRESENCE IN THE MIDST OF THE CONVERSATION AS GOD BEGINS TO SPEAK TO YOU DURING PRAYER.**

Take a moment now. Center and quiet yourself. Listen in your head to hear your voice as God begins to speak to you through you. Here is a little help. When you start this exercise, you may first hear silly, stupid, or even anti-Christ statements. You may hear evil things. Do not consider these initial words to be the voice of God. The evil one will try to invade your mind by sending evil thoughts. These thoughts will always be in competition with the voice of God in your life. Do not allow them to get you off track. Don't let them stop you from listening. Power through them in order to begin hearing directly from God.

There is a way for you to tell when God is speaking through you and to you. You will begin to experience a peaceful and godly presence in the midst of the conversation. Anticipate this and welcome it. Do not stop until you experience this.

Go ahead and begin this exercise. When you begin to hear from God, write down what you hear Him saying to you.

_____

_____

_____

_____

_____

_____

If we can accept the truth that a prophet is able to speak to us in his or her own voice directly from God, we should easily grasp the truth that we are also able to speak in our own voice directly from God. If we believe that it is possible to receive a prophecy through someone else, we should also believe that we can receive a prophecy from our own voice. That's right! Don't be afraid to prophesy to yourself. Whenever God is speaking through us, and the message is for us, we are prophesying to ourselves. What a blessing this is to know! You may think that you are just speaking in your head. You may think that you are just talking to yourself. You may even think that your mind is speaking to you. No! When it comes to the things of God and the fruit of the Spirit, it is God speaking to you and through you.

> **WHENEVER GOD IS SPEAKING THROUGH US, AND THE MESSAGE IS FOR US, WE ARE PROPHESYING TO OURSELVES.**

An important point to remember is that we can't create a prophecy from within ourselves on our own. We shouldn't say that the voice we heard originated in our own minds. Did you get that? God has even wired us to not be able to fool ourselves.

WE CAN'T CREATE A PROPHECY FROM WITHIN OURSELVES ON OUR OWN.

We can't trick ourselves into speaking a prophecy even if we tried. To prove this truth, look at 2 Peter 1:21:

> For prophecy never had its origin in the human will, but prophets, though human, spoke from God as they were carried along by the Holy Spirit.

Do you see it? Did you grasp this truth? Scripture plainly and clearly states that prophecy *never* had its origin in *the will of man*. It goes on to say that when a man would speak, he did not speak on his own or from his own mind. Man spoke from God. In other words, the message originated from God, as they were under the direction of the Holy Spirit.

Therefore, go ahead, prophesy to yourself based on what you hear God saying to you. Listen to what He has to say about your life! Listen to what He has to say about your finances! Listen to what He has to say about your job, marriage, children, home, and church. Listen, and then let Him speak His thoughts through you. Be assured that when His thoughts are expressed through you, they will come to pass. Remember, this is not something that originated within you. It originated from God. Therefore, if God has said it, it is done, in the name of Christ Jesus. What a blessing!

THE WORDS OF GOD MUST ORIGINATE FROM HIM, NOT US.

Again, the key truth here is to remember that the words of God must originate from Him, not us. How, then, do we make sure of that? How do we make sure that we are not forcing our will into a prayer? The answer is that we must surrender our will to God every single time we enter prayer. Surrendering our will to conform to God's will is the ultimate form of humility that we can show our heavenly Father.

Ephesians 5:17 says:

Therefore do not be foolish, but understand what the Lord's will is.

This is a key truth for us to understand in order to make sure that our prayers receive their life and strength from God. We must be sure that we understand what the Lord's will is concerning certain issues in our lives. By hearing Him speak to us, and through us, we may discover that we are facing challenges in our lives that have nothing to do with falling short of His grace or anything that we have done wrong. It may be God's will to allow us to experience something challenging in order to get to the blessing He has for us.

Most people don't like this kind of talk, but there are times when we must walk a more challenging path than we would prefer in order for certain parts of our character, demeanor, and attitude to be shaped and conformed into the image of Christ.

> THERE ARE TIMES WHEN WE MUST WALK A MORE CHALLENGING PATH THAN WE WOULD PREFER IN ORDER FOR CERTAIN PARTS OF OUR CHARACTER, DEMEANOR, AND ATTITUDE TO BE SHAPED AND CONFORMED INTO THE IMAGE OF CHRIST.

Here is another great secret to life: It is not getting what you want that is important, but being able to hold on to it after you get it. Our ability to hold on to something, and have peace after we obtain it, is the key to our happiness on earth. We must learn that getting things is often the easiest part. Keeping them without losing our minds, our peace, and our tranquility can be the more challenging part. This is why God sometimes chooses to take us through a more challenging path on our way to achieving His purpose in our lives.

Would you rather face unexpected challenging times unprepared? Or would you rather know that challenges will come your way, and be prepared for them, knowing that Christ is with you to bring you peace in the process of fulfilling God's purpose? There is comfort in knowing that God will prophesy through us and to us by showing us the challenges that are destined to come at us in life. Our comfort is the confidence that comes from knowing that He will bring us peace and patience to endure those challenges. And, that we will become better off after going through the process.

> THERE IS COMFORT IN KNOWING THAT GOD WILL PROPHESY THROUGH US AND TO US BY SHOWING US THE CHALLENGES THAT ARE DESTINED TO COME AT US IN LIFE.

There is no better display of this than what is written in 2 Corinthians 4:16–18:

Therefore we do not lose heart. Though outwardly we are wasting away, yet inwardly we are being renewed day by day. For our light and momentary troubles are achieving for us an eternal glory that far outweighs them all. So we fix our eyes not on what is seen, but on what is unseen, since what is seen is temporary, but what is unseen is eternal.

We are inwardly renewed every day through prayer, by which God will let us know what to expect and how to deal with it. We might be praying one day, and God speaks through us and to us, saying, "Look at 2 Corinthians 4:16–18." He may let us know that this Scripture is intended for us to be able to handle unforeseen circumstances in the next several weeks. If we casually read over it and immediately become turned off by it, we will miss the blessing in the passage that God wants us to understand.

Go ahead, look at 2 Corinthians 4:16–18 again. After looking at it again, you may ask yourself, *What is the blessing for me in this Scripture?* You may even go on to wonder, *I sure don't see any blessing in this Scripture.* Well, I am here to tell you this passage of Scripture is loaded with blessings.

Notice what *"troubles"* have been designed to do. If you continue to look at these verses, I promise that they will begin to open up to you, just like heaven opened for Christ in Luke 3:21. Literally, when Scripture opens up to you, heaven is opening up as well. Again, Scripture opens up because heaven opens up. Why? Because the voice of God will begin to speak to you, through you! Just as heaven opened and the voice of God from heaven spoke to Jesus, the same thing will happen as we meditate on this passage of Scripture.

Read it again:

> *Therefore we do not lose heart. Though outwardly we are wasting away, yet inwardly we are being renewed day by day. For our light and momentary troubles are achieving for us an eternal glory that far outweighs them all. So we fix our eyes not on what is seen, but on what is unseen, since what is seen is temporary, but what is unseen is eternal.*

We commonly view *troubles* as terrible things. But look at what the Bible says about troubles. The Scripture says troubles are *"light and momentary."* Did you get this? Do you see it? Troubles are viewed by God as *"light."* In other words, troubles are something that God designed for us to be able to carry. We can carry all our troubles easily, as long as we present them to Christ Jesus. He converts them in the natural so that they become lighter burdens for us. They become lighter as we share them with Him.

Matthew 11:29–30 supports this truth.

Take my yoke upon you and learn from me, for I am gentle and humble in heart, and you will find rest for your souls. For my yoke is easy and my burden is light.

Many people make the mistake of thinking that if they can just carry their burdens to the Lord and leave them there, all will be okay. We may even think that we won't have to deal with that particular trouble anymore. This is wrong thinking. The truth is that when we carry our troubles or burdens to the Lord, they may not always immediately leave us. However, there is joy in knowing that Christ will become one with us—yoked to us—and He will help us carry the load of our burdens. Christ will share the load of our burdens until God has allowed trouble to run its course in our lives.

Now you may be asking, "What good are troubles to me?" Well, first, they are designed to be momentary. Troubles are not supposed to last. They are only momentary.

Second Corinthians 4:17 says,

For our light and momentary troubles are achieving for us an eternal glory that far outweighs them all.

Second, let's focus on the reason and purpose of troubles in our lives. Troubles are designed to achieve for us a greater glory in Christ. Troubles have been designed by God to help us achieve a greater glory in Him. Look at the verse above. Knowing this truth, we should welcome a direct word from God that reveals to us the challenging times ahead. It should be okay with us that things get a little difficult from time to time. As long as we know we have the presence and power of Christ in our lives, not just to overcome them, but also to grow and strengthen us from challenging times, we should not live in fear of troubles. What a blessing from God.

Why, then, do we become nervous, upset, and scared when we are faced with these challenges? Perhaps it is because we forget the word that came to us in prayer: *"So we fix our eyes not on what is seen, but on what is unseen. For what is seen is temporary, but what is unseen is eternal."*

How do we get to this point? How can we stay focused on our blessing in the midst of the storm? We must learn to pray with our eyes open, looking up to heaven, and training ourselves to be able to see unseen things that are eternal instead of the momentary things that are temporary. What a blessing it is when we are able to see the unseen realities of the goodness of God and the fruit of the Holy Spirit!

> ## WHAT A BLESSING IT IS WHEN WE ARE ABLE TO SEE THE UNSEEN REALITIES OF THE GOODNESS OF GOD AND THE FRUIT OF THE HOLY SPIRIT!

Even Christ Jesus, enduring all the ridicule and evil things that happened to Him as He was nailed to the cross, did not come down, because He saw something no one else could see. He saw the one thing that kept Him going through the pain, hurt, and disappointment: joy. Hebrews 12:2 reveals this truth:

Fixing our eyes on Jesus, the pioneer and perfecter of our faith. For the joy set before him he endured the cross, scorning its shame, and sat down at the right hand of the throne of God.

Yes! Joy was set before Him, before He even got up on the cross. Joy was there waiting on Him, before He ever stretched out His arms. It was joy that placed Him there, and joy that kept Him up there. What was this joy He knew about? It was knowing that we would have eternal life because we would always believe in Him and what He has done for us. We would know that He died for our sins. And we would have everlasting life by committing our lives to Him and His cause. What a blessing that is for us to know!

Joy to the world! The Lord has come! Let earth redeem her King!

CHAPTER 7: KEY POINT REVIEW

1. Prayer is *the* method God uses to communicate whatever He wants, whenever He wants.

2. We should stay alert and watchful of God to speak to us and through us with truth, purpose, and power.

3. God will use the Holy Spirit to speak on His behalf in the form of your own voice.

4. You will begin to experience a peaceful and godly presence in the midst of the conversation as God begins to speak to you during prayer.

5. Whenever God is speaking through us, and the message is for us, we are prophesying to ourselves.

6. We can't create a prophecy from within ourselves on our own.

7. The words of God must originate from Him, not us.

8. There are times when we must walk a more challenging path than we would prefer in order for certain parts of our character, demeanor, and attitude to be shaped and conformed into the image of Christ.

9. There is comfort in knowing that God will prophesy through us and to us by showing us the challenges that are destined to come at us in life.

10. What a blessing it is when we are able to see the unseen realities of the goodness of God and the fruit of the Holy Spirit!

SPIRITUAL EXERCISE

1. Write down the things you want God to reveal to you about being able to sense when change is taking place during your personal prayer time.

_____

_____

_____

_____

_____

_____

_____

2. Write down any insights you learned in this chapter.

_____

_____

_____

_____

_____

_____

_____

8

MEDITATE UNTIL YOU SEE YOUR BLESSING

My eyes stay open through the watches of the night, that I may meditate on your promises.
—Psalm 119:148

We know by now that God answers our prayers. He will answer us because He cares for us and loves us. However, we need to understand that when He answers us, it could be something He wants us to know now about a future time. There are times when God's answer comes to us in the form of a promise. These are those occasions in which God speaks to you and tells you that He is going to do something, but that something is going to occur at a later date. That can be frustrating to hear. Most of us love it when God speaks to us, but we don't like it when His answers come in the form of a future promise.

> **THERE ARE TIMES WHEN GOD'S ANSWER COMES TO US IN THE FORM OF A PROMISE.**

One of the reasons we are not happy about promises is because we have to faithfully wait for them to manifest in our lives. They don't happen immediately after our prayer, but rest assured, they *will* come to pass. Maybe if we understood the power behind God's promises, we would be more willing to wait on His blessings to manifest in our lives at the time He ordains for them to occur.

> **THE PROMISE IS NOT MADE TO US, IT IS MADE FOR US.
> IN OTHER WORDS, GOD SPEAKS TO HIS WORDS,
> AND THEY MUST DO WHAT HE SAYS.**

In the New Testament, the word *promise* is derived from the Greek word *epaggelia*, which means "a summons." Merriam-Webster defines the word *summons* as "a call by authority to appear at a place named or to attend to a duty…at a day specified." Thus, when God promises that He is going to do something, a specific order has been given. Please pay special attention that the promise is not made *to* us, but it is made *for* us. In other words, God speaks His words and they must do what He says. He literally commissions, or summons, His words to do something for Him, and they must do what they have been summoned to do.

Isaiah 55:9–11 says,

> *As the heavens are higher than the earth, so are my ways higher than your ways and my thoughts than your thoughts. As the rain and the snow come down from heaven, and do not return to it without watering the earth and making it bud and flourish, so that it yields seed for the sower and bread for the eater, so is my word that goes out from my mouth: it will not return to me empty, but will accomplish what I desire and achieve the purpose for which I sent it.*

Again, we can see clearly now how God summons His Word to appear at certain places, expects His Word to perform certain tasks, and anticipates His Word returning to Him, having achieved the purpose for which the Word was sent. This key point is outstanding for us to know. And, it helps us rest in prayer, knowing that God will do exactly what He promises for us. We just need to have the assurance that what He says will happen at the appointed time.

> **WHEN WE RECEIVE AN ANSWER FROM GOD IN PRAYER, THE HARDEST PART FOR US IS WAITING WITH THE ASSURANCE AND CONFIDENCE THAT WHAT HE SAID WILL BE DONE.**

When we receive an answer from God in the form of a promise, the hardest part for us is waiting with the assurance and confidence that what He said will be done will, in fact, come to pass. But there is hope for us in Scripture, which helps us to have peace and gives us the ability to wait with patience and confidence. By focusing on Scripture, we are able to *meditate* on God's promises. Meditation is a truth revealed that allows us to maintain peace, assurance, and patience as we wait for God's promises to show up in our lives.

> **MEDITATION IS A TRUTH REVEALED THAT ALLOWS US TO MAINTAIN PEACE, ASSURANCE, AND PATIENCE AS WE WAIT FOR GOD'S PROMISES TO SHOW UP IN OUR LIVES.**

Psalm 119:148 says,

My eyes stay open through the watches of the night, that I may meditate on your promises.

It is only through the truth principle of meditation that a promise spoken by God can manifest to us. The psalmist says that he meditates throughout the night at assigned times to make sure that he remains focused on all the promises that God has spoken to him. He wants to do his part to make sure that what God has promised him will come to him. Hebrews 11:6 says, *"Without faith it is impossible to please God, because… he rewards those who earnestly seek him."* And we know that faith comes from hearing, or meditating, on God's Word. (See Romans 10:17.) Thus, a key point for us to learn here, and never forget, is that meditation releases God's ability to work on your behalf.

Ask most people what meditation means and he or she will probably begin to describe a person sitting in a cross-legged position, hands opened, eyes closed, and making humming sounds. This is a type of mediation that empties the mind. Scripture, however, clearly defines for us what meditation is and how to do it. *"Cause me to understand the way of your precepts, that I may **meditate** on your wonderful deeds"* (Psalm 1:2).

Here we can see that our meditation should be focused on the law of the Lord. The law of the Lord is whatever God has summoned or promised for us. Please note that Scripture says we are to direct our meditative focus on the law of the Lord, or the words spoken by the Lord.

MEDITATION SHOULD BE FOCUSED ON THE LAW OF THE LORD.

Now, let's define meditation in a very deep level to grasp this truth. The Hebrew word translated as *"meditates"* is *siyach*, meaning "to meditate upon, study, ponder." The *Theological Wordbook of the Old Testament* says that the "basic meaning of this verb seems to be 'rehearse', 'repent', or 'go over a matter in one's mind.'"[2]

---

2. See http://www.thyword.ca/meditate.html (accessed February 1, 2018).

Thus we have:

STAGES OF MEDITATION

Pondering God's Promises in Our Minds

↓

Repent by Changing Our Minds

↓

Rehearse What God Has Said He Will Do

So, meditation is more of a progressive response to a promise from God than an isolated exercise that we do to feel better or release stress. First, we must go over in our mind what God has said He will do. We literally have to ponder or deeply think about what He said. Deeply thinking about what God said means we must go over that particular promise in our minds. We must always remember that if our minds can't comprehend and accept what God has promised, nothing can show up for us. Our minds must focus on His promises and realize that they are for the fulfilling of God's purpose through our lives.

> **MEDITATION IS MORE OF A PROGRESSIVE RESPONSE TO A PROMISE FROM GOD THAN AN ISOLATED EXERCISE THAT WE DO TO FEEL BETTER OR RELEASE STRESS.**

We must further know that God's promises spoken to us will always place us in His perfect will. It is when we ponder God's perfect promises in our minds that we remove all doubt and confusion about what He said He will do.

> **IT IS WHEN WE PONDER GOD'S PERFECT PROMISES IN OUR MINDS THAT WE REMOVE ALL DOUBT AND CONFUSION ABOUT WHAT HE SAID HE WILL DO.**

We can then rest assured that we are in His perfect will. Romans 12:2 says,

> *Do not conform to the pattern of this world, but be transformed by the renewing of your mind. Then you will be able to test and approve what God's will is—his good, pleasing and perfect will.*

Meditating on God's promises renews our minds to the things God wants to give to us and do through us. *"Renewing"* means "a renovation, complete change for the better." It is to restore us to a place where we can tap into the purposes of God, by which we are renewed in our strength, confidence, and hope. We begin to operate in a more vigorous and energetic manner as we do our daily tasks, knowing that we are productive in fulfilling God's purpose for our lives. Let's not forget that the key here is to make sure we renew our minds on the promises of God by thoroughly focusing on what He said He wants to do through us.

> *The kingdom of God has come near. **Repent** and believe the good news!* (Mark 1:15)

The next stage of meditation is the repenting stage. The word *repent* (in Greek, *metanoeo*) is often used in the context of changing one's behavior or ceasing to do a bad thing, but the Greek word means "to change one's mind." The apostle Paul urged, *"Do not conform to the pattern of this world, but be transformed by the renewing of your mind"* (Romans 12:2). Renewal doesn't come from a change of behavior but from a new way of thinking. Once our minds have been renewed, we must think our way into going in a new direction.

ONCE OUR MINDS HAVE BEEN RENEWED, WE MUST THINK OUR WAY INTO GOING IN A NEW DIRECTION.

We can't go back to our old way of thinking once we have been given a newness of thought. We will be tempted to fall into doubt, fear, and guilt as we begin to execute the promises of God. Issues and circumstances may come to us, and we will be tempted to revert to our old way of thinking on how to deal with these issues. We must know that we are new creations in Christ, and that our minds have been renewed through meditation. We must fight off the urge to use our old ways of solving problems. We must allow our renewed mind to show us God's way of dealing with unforeseen circumstances. Thus, it is the repenting, or changing from the way we do things, that becomes difficult for us. It is hard to try a new way to solve old problems. However, when we repent and lean on God's newness, which has been placed in our minds, we will experience positive results as we progress in fulfilling His purpose in our lives.

This truth is illustrated in Ephesians 4:22–24, which says,

You were taught, with regard to your former way of life, to put off your old self, which is being corrupted by its deceitful desires; to be made new in the attitude of your minds; and to put on the new self, created to be like God in true righteousness and holiness.

We can see the importance of having a new attitude in our minds, which can only come through proper meditation in prayer. Finally, after pondering God's Word and repenting, we must rehearse His promises to prepare us for what is to come.

AFTER PONDERING GOD'S WORD AND REPENTING, WE MUST REHEARSE HIS PROMISES TO PREPARE US FOR WHAT IS TO COME.

Again, Psalm 119:148 says,

My eyes stay open through the watches of the night, that I may meditate on your promises.

And Psalm 45:1 says,

My heart is stirred by a noble theme as I recite my verses for the king; my tongue is the pen of a skillful writer.

From these two Scriptures, we discover that we must remain diligent to continue the practice of meditation, even through the night. We are to continuously recite the themes of what God has promised us.

When we think of the word *rehearse*, we must not miss the power that is there for us to grasp. When an actor lands a role in a movie, he or she has a script. The director knows the beginning and end of the movie. The director knows the overall theme that he or she wants to bring out. The actor must rehearse lines from the script to know what to say at the right time so these themes will be portrayed as planned. By rehearsing the lines, the actor is prepared to correctly recite them at the proper time so that the movie is successful and the proper themes are presented. As much as the director knows the theme of the movie, the script and the outcome, the movie will not be successful if the actors don't rehearse their lines.

It is the same way for us in life. The Holy Spirit is the director of our lives, and God the Father has written a script for us to follow. That script is revealed to us in the words of Christ Jesus, through the Holy Spirit, for us to recite. As we recite and rehearse the words and promises from God, our lives take on a theme of victory, success, and purpose.

However, special care must be taken to remember that we are reciting God's promises so that our minds will continuously be engaged with the reality of what He said will come to pass. Our repeating of what God has promised is not meant to rush Him in delivering those promises. Our repeating of God's promises builds and demonstrates our trust and hope in Him. When God sees our faith grow as we meditate on His promises, He then knows that we have faith to see them manifest in our lives.

Again, it is the meditation process of prayer in which we ponder His words in our minds, repent from our old ways of thinking, and rehearse what we know will happen, that will bring His promises to life.

Practice the first stage of meditation by focusing your mind on what God has promised you. Think deeply about it. Turn it over in your mind and write your thoughts below.

_____

_____

_____

_____

_____

_____

Now, proceed to the second stage of meditation, in which you repent, or change from your old way of thinking about how you will fulfill the part you must play in seeing God's promises come to fruition in your life. In other words, write down how you will…

+ Deal with unforeseen circumstances concerning His promises…

+ Take a new approach to letting Him work through you to fulfill His promises…

✦ And surrender your old way of doing things as you begin to walk in a new way of trusting Him to fulfill His will in your life.

_____

_____

_____

_____

_____

_____

_____

Finally, in the last stage of meditation, write down the promises you are to rehearse during the day and night as they come to your remembrance.

_____

_____

_____

_____

_____

_____

_____

CHAPTER 8: REVIEW AND EXERCISE

1. There are times when God's answer comes to us in the form of a promise.

2. God's promise is not made *to* us, but it is made *for* us. In other words, God speaks His words and they must do what He says.

3. When we receive an answer from God in prayer, the hardest part for us is waiting with the assurance and confidence that what He said will be done.

4. Meditation is a truth revealed that allows us to maintain peace, assurance, and patience as we wait for God's promises to show up in our lives.

5. Meditation should be focused on the law of the Lord.

6. Meditation is more of a progressive response to a promise from God than an isolated exercise that we do to feel better or release stress.

7. It is when we ponder God's perfect promises in our minds that we remove all doubt and confusion about what He said He will do.

8. Once our minds have been renewed, we must think our way into going in a new direction.

9. After pondering God's Word and repenting, we must rehearse His promises to prepare us for what is to come.

SPIRITUAL EXERCISE

1. Write down the things you want God to reveal to you about being able to sense when change is taking place during your personal prayer time.

_____

_____

_____

_____

_____

_____

_____

2. Write down any insights you learned in this chapter.

_____

_____

_____

_____

_____

_____

_____

9

GET READY TO OPEN HEAVEN

By getting to this point of the book, you have hopefully reached a new level of prayer in which heaven will open up for you, again and again. You have completed several exercises and learned many new truths. Now, we must put all the pieces together.

Prayer can seem like a nebulous and overwhelming experience unless you approach it in a properly structured way. In essence, prayer is the simple act of communication between you and God, with the help of Jesus and the Holy Spirit. Let's summarize the truths from each chapter, and then come up with a strategy so that your prayers can cause heaven to open each and every time you pray.

THE EIGHT TRUTHS THAT OPEN HEAVEN

Truth 1: As we pray, heaven opens up for us.

Truth 2: We should expect change to occur within us immediately as we are praying.

Truth 3: God answers our prayers before we pray.

Truth 4: We must reach a level of stillness in prayer in order for God to act on our behalf.

Truth 5: When we pray from our hearts, we reach God's heart.

Truth 6: The Holy Spirit intercedes for us to allow us the opportunity to say the perfect prayer that only our Father can hear.

Truth 7: God speaks to us, through us.

Truth 8: The promises of God are revealed to us through meditation.

TRUTH 1: *AS WE PRAY, HEAVEN OPENS UP FOR US.*

We must never forget this truth. We must envision heaven opening up each time we pray. We must get a mental picture of heaven opening as we look toward the ceiling. Until the vision forms, we should keep looking up, and eventually the vision of heaven opening will form. Remember the cube exercise? As we stared at the drawing of a cube, it began to rotate and move to show different openings. That is the same way heaven opens for us. Heaven opens as we stare and focus on the clouds and sky above us. It literally will open up for us right in front of our eyes.

TRUTH 2: *WE SHOULD EXPECT CHANGE TO OCCUR WITHIN US IMMEDIATELY AS WE ARE PRAYING.*

That's right. We should expect inward and outward changes to occur in the process of our actual prayer. Our disposition should change first. In other words, our mood and emotions should positively change during our time of prayer. Next, we should expect an outward change to occur for us as well. If Jesus's clothes can change on the Mount of Transfiguration (see Mark 9:2–9), then we should know that everything we come into contact with will change as well.

Don't forget that as we are praying, we should experience "The Nine Prayer Points of Completeness." They begin with physical sensations as we experience God's presence. Once His presence is felt in our natural bodies, it then changes our mental and emotional states. Our emotional state is the critical point in which we develop a more positive outlook on life. After we have developed a positive outlook on life, our mood becomes positive as well. This defines our character, or the way people perceive us based on how we act. Finally, our character creates the type of attitude that we display to everyone we encounter. Our attitudes also determine how we approach and handle any challenges we may face.

TRUTH 3: *GOD ANSWERS OUR PRAYERS BEFORE WE PRAY.*

God has prepared all the answers to our prayers before we even pray. He moves on us, giving us the desire to pray so that we will ask Him the right questions that can release His preordained answers in our time of need. The questions we ask in prayer are designed by the Father and allow His answers to address any decisions, issues or circumstances we face. Prayer is the way in which God has chosen for His answers to be revealed to us.

TRUTH 4: *WE MUST REACH A LEVEL OF STILLNESS IN PRAYER IN ORDER FOR GOD TO ACT ON OUR BEHALF.*

Too often, we are busy, nervous, and rushed when it comes to prayer. It is in our stillness that we become centered on God and on His goodness. We must strive to reach the deepest level of stillness when we pray to God. There are four levels of stillness that we must understand how to reach.

Stillness can be achieved by focusing on our own inhaling and exhaling breathing exercises. When you can reach a point in the exercise in which you can experience God's presence and feel completely connected with Him, you have reached the *first level* of stillness. When your thoughts become peaceful and heavenly, you have reached the *second level* of stillness. When you become aware of only the presence of God and nothing or no one else, you have reached the *third level* of stillness. You are now ready to hear God speak and watch Him take action on your behalf. This is the *fourth and deepest level* of stillness.

TRUTH 5: *WHEN WE PRAY FROM OUR HEARTS, WE REACH GOD'S HEART.*

What a beautiful truth to know. Our heartfelt prayers move on God's heart and blessings flow from heaven. A heart-led prayer allows us to pray *in time*, pray *in truth*, and pray *on point*.

Praying *in time* means to be aware of the truth that God has allowed a certain window of time for us to connect with Him uniquely. We then must pray *in truth* by simply opening up our hearts and praying from within ourselves with all our might. If we speak to God in truth, the connection is quickly made and heaven opens. Praying *on point* means that we must know the right words to say to God. In other words, we must know the precise truth to speak to Him about. We pray on point when we don't jump and skip around as we pray to God. When we become still and centered, our hearts become engaged to God's heart. As a result, our hearts then open up, and we can speak truthfully to Him.

TRUTH 6: *THE HOLY SPIRIT INTERCEDES FOR US TO ALLOW US THE OPPORTUNITY TO SAY THE PERFECT PRAYER THAT ONLY OUR FATHER CAN HEAR.*

The Holy Spirit intercedes for us when we don't know what to say in our prayers. The Holy Spirit intervenes during prayer to listen to both sides as witness to what is being said. The Holy Spirit blocks any parts of the prayer from anyone who shouldn't hear what is being said between you and God. Finally, the Holy Spirit brings our prayers in line with God's will so that they are heard and answered by God only.

TRUTH 7: *GOD SPEAKS TO US, THROUGH US.*

Second Samuel 23:2 says, *"The Spirit of the LORD spoke through me; his word was on my tongue."* The Lord can speak through us and instruct us about what to say. In other words, when God is speaking to us, we may be speaking in our own voice but it is God who is directing what we are saying. He is speaking *through* us, not just *to* us. When we hear a peaceful, godly voice in our head talking, we must not say, "Something told me...." We must now say, "The Holy Spirit told me..." or "God told me...." Finally, our tongues should be under the authority of God, and opened to be used by Him however He wants to use them. This is what happens when someone prophesies to us. They may speaking to us in their own voice, but in reality, it is God speaking to us through them.

TRUTH 8: *THE PROMISES OF GOD ARE REVEALED TO US THROUGH MEDITATION.*

Meditation is more of a progressive response to a promise from God than an isolated exercise that we do to feel better or release stress. First, we must rehearse the promises of God—what He has said He will do—in our minds. We need to deeply reflect on what He has said. Deeply thinking about what God has said means that we must repeat that particular promise in our minds, over and over again.

We must always remember that if our minds can't comprehend and accept what God has promised, then answers to our prayers will not materialize for us. Our minds must focus on God's promises and realize that these promises are for the fulfilling of His purpose in our lives. We must further know that God's promises spoken to us will always place us in His perfect will. When we ponder God's perfect promises in our minds, we remove all doubt and confusion about what He has said He will do.

HOW TO GET HEAVEN TO OPEN WHEN WE PRAY

Now that we know the eight truths that will open up heaven for us in prayer, how do we put it all together? Here are the steps we should take to ensure that heaven will open for us when we pray.

Step 1: Mentally envision heaven opening up to you. As you pray, it will happen. Before we begin our prayer, we must mentally imagine heaven opening up. Keep on praying until it happens.

Step 2: As we pray, we should expect change to occur immediately. Once we begin to pray and are in the act of praying, we should expect an inward and outward change to occur in the process of our prayer. If you don't feel a change in your demeanor, keep trying until it happens.

Step 3: As you feel drawn to prayer, God is ready to reveal answers to you about circumstances you face. We must know that it is really God who is drawing us to prayer. He has answers for us that He wants to reveal to us through prayer.

Step 4: You must still yourself in order to be able to connect and hear from God. We must reach the deepest level of *stillness* where we will be able to connect with God and get ready to hear from Him.

Step 5: We can confidently pray from our heart to God's heart as heaven opens up. Once we connect with God, it is then that our hearts will reach God's heart. God will then become attentive to our prayers and move on our behalf.

Step 6: The Holy Spirit will intercede for us and help us pray the perfect prayer every time. The Holy Spirit will begin to intercede for us as we commune with God. He will make us pray the perfect prayer to God every time. As we approach this part of prayer, we must be confident that we can pray the perfect prayer from our heart as the Holy Spirit will assist us in saying the right things to God.

Step 7: We should get ready to hear God speak to us, through us. We can expect God to begin to answer us. He will begin to talk to us and direct us.

Step 8: He may speak in the form of a promise that can only be manifested through meditation. We must understand that sometimes He will answer us in the form of a promise. A promise from God is a guarantee that He will do something through us for the purpose He has for our lives. Promises are different than answers in that they are something commissioned to happen at a specific time. We must meditate on what He promises us until His promises appear at His appointed time.

When we can grasp these steps based on the eight truths that open heaven and practice them in our actual prayer time, we will see heaven open and deliver the good things of God.

CHAPTER 9: SPIRITUAL EXERCISES

1. Write down the eight truths of prayer that open heaven.

_____

_____

_____

_____

_____

_____

_____

2. Next, write down the eight steps we must go through in prayer in order to get heaven to open.

_____

_____

_____

_____

_____

_____

_____

_____

3. Finally, write down a heart-felt prayer to God asking Him to move on your heart to master all truths taught in this book so that you can have a more powerful prayer life.

_____

_____

_____

_____

_____

_____

_____

_____

_____

_____

_____

_____

_____

_____

_____

_____

_____

_____

EPILOGUE

One of the surest ways to experience prayers that will open heaven for you is to accept Christ Jesus as your Lord and Savior. If you have never done this, repeat these simple words with me and it will be a done deal. Repeat with me the following: Lord Christ Jesus as of this very moment, I accept you as Lord and savior of my life. I now give my life to you to be fashioned for your purpose and glory. All these things I have said I truly believe in my heart and have confessed with my mouth. I know now that I have received ever-lasting life based on the work that Christ will do in my life. Lord Christ, thank you for bringing me to this point of my life where I surrender all to you. It is in the Holy Spirit through Christ Jesus I say Amen.

Humbly Yours in Christ,
Apostle Jamie Pleasant

ABOUT THE AUTHOR

Jamie T. Pleasant is the chief executive pastor and founder of New Zion Christian Church in Suwanee, Georgia. As a modern-day polymath, he holds a bachelor's degree in physics from Benedict College in Columbia, South Carolina, a bachelor's degree in marketing studies from Clemson University, and an MBA in marketing from Clark Atlanta University. In 1999, Jamie achieved a Georgia Tech milestone by becoming the first African-American to graduate with a PhD in business management in the school's 110-plus-year history.

God gave Jamie the vision to establish a biblically based economic development initiative for New Zion Christian Church, and he remains at the pulse of the economic business sector. He has created cutting-edge and industry-leading ministerial programs in the church, such as the Financial Literacy Academy for Youth (FLAFY), Wealth Builders Investment Club (WBIC), and the Institute of Entrepreneurship (IOE). The newly added SAT and PSAT prep courses for children ages nine to nineteen fuels the potential success of all who walk through the doors of New Zion Christian Church. Jamie has met with political officials such as President Clinton and former South African President

Nelson Mandela, and he has performed marriage ceremonies for and counseled numerous celebrated personalities, such as Usher Raymond (Confessions Recording Artist), Terri Vaughn (Lavita Jenkins on *The Steve Harvey Show*), and many others.

Apostle Pleasant is a member of Alpha Phi Alpha and husband of Kimberly Pleasant (whom he loves dearly) and the proud father of three children: Christian, Zion, and Nacara.

Welcome to Our House!

We Have a Special Gift for You

It is our privilege and pleasure to share in your love of Christian books. We are committed to bringing you authors and books that feed, challenge, and enrich your faith.

To show our appreciation, we invite you to sign up to receive a specially selected **Reader Appreciation Gift**, with our compliments. Just go to the Web address at the bottom of this page.

God bless you as you seek a deeper walk with Him!

WE HAVE A GIFT FOR YOU. VISIT:

whpub.me/nonfictionthx

WHITAKER
HOUSE